MOTHER EARTH

SUNSET AND REFLECTED MOONRISE, CRATER LAKE AND WIZARD ISLAND. CRATER LAKE NATIONAL PARK, OREGON. KATHLEEN NORRIS COOK.

SIERRA CLUB BOOKS SAN FRANCISCO

Mother Earth

Through the Eyes of Women Photographers and Writers

Edited by Judith Boice

The Sierra Club, founded in 1892 by John Muir, has devoted itself to the study and protection of the earth's scenic and ecological resources—mountains, wetlands, woodlands, wild shores and rivers, deserts and plains. The publishing program of the Sierra Club offers books to the public as a nonprofit educational service in the hope that they may enlarge the public's understanding of the Club's basic concerns. The point of view expressed in each book, however, does not necessarily represent that of the Club. The Sierra Club has some sixty chapters coast to coast, in Canada, Hawaii, and Alaska. For information about how you may participate in its programs to preserve wilderness and the quality of life, please address inquiries to Sierra Club, 730 Polk Street, San Francisco, CA 94109.

LIBRARY OF CONGRESS CATALOGING-IN-PUBLICATION DATA
Mother Earth : through the eyes of women photographers and writers /
edited by Judith Boice.
p. cm.
ISBN 0-87156-556-0 :
1. Landscape photography. I. Boice, Judith, 1962– .
TR660.5.M68   1992   92-1143
779'.082—dc20   CIP

Editor: David Spinner
Editorial Consultant: Linda Gunnarson
Production by Janet Vail
Cover design by Paula Schlosser
Book design by Paula Schlosser
Composition by Harrington-Young Typography

Printed in Hong Kong

10   9   8   7   6   5   4   3

CONTENTS

To my mother, Martha Hibbert Boice;
and her mother, Gladys Harbage Hibbert (1897–1990);
and all of my ancestors linking me back to
the Mother of All Things.

Acknowledgements

My thanks to the impassioned women photographers and writers who have offered freely of their inspiration and encouragement.

My gratitude to Linda Gunnarson for her capable, visionary work in shaping the book. Special thanks to David Spinner, Jon Beckmann, and the staff at Sierra Club Books for their guidance and assistance in bringing the book into form.

Thanks to the Elements—Earth, Air, Fire, and Water—the foundation of all Creation, including the pages you hold in your hands.

My gratitude to the three Graces—Algaia (Brilliance), Euphrosyne (Joy), and Thalia (Bloom)—who infuse the Elements with elegance and beauty.

Thanks to Gaia, Mother Earth, my ongoing source of inspiration and support— may these words and images honor your strength and beauty.

INTRODUCTION

Judith Boice

MOTHER EARTH: THROUGH THE EYES OF WOMEN *Photographers and Writers* presents a view of our planet that is drawn from many women's journeys. My goal with this collection of photographs and writings is to inspire people with the beauty of the Earth. I offer photographic images to feed the heart. Visual images have the power to bypass the logical mind and make a direct impression on the soul. Accompanying the photographs are selections from women's writings about the Earth. These words are meant to enhance the images, not to overwhelm them. I offer these words to feed the mind, to open new doorways of perception. Concepts communicated through words have the power to change the way that we perceive and thus the way that we see the world, and ultimately to alter the way that we interact with the world as well.

My own explorations on four continents opened my eyes and heart to view the Earth differently, to see the common threads that bind this diverse planet into an intricate pattern of wholeness. Beauty emerged as one unifying thread in that weave. The beauty of the planet touched and changed me in ways that intellectual information never could, and through its power I became a lover of wildness, of unfettered aliveness, and a devotee of the vast repository of wisdom inherent in the Earth.

During my journeys I came to speak more of "Earth" and less of "nature." Too often in our culture the word "nature" refers to all that is not human or human-made. We tend to view nature as something separate from our daily existence, a passing amusement for weekends or extended holiday trips. We lose sight that we humans are a part of the whole of creation. Sometimes we are belligerent participants, bent on asserting our illusory independence from the web of life. We are "bloody in tooth and claw," the epitome of Darwin's predatory "survival of the fittest" paradigm. But the hard facts of science are in truth soft, malleable as putty, and scientists now postulate that evolution favors species that most actively support the ecosystem and bypasses self-serving organisms. Human disconnection from the Earth, actively encouraged from the time of the Industrial Revolution to the present, has made possible the rampant destruction of the Earth's resources and weakened the planet's vitality—and ultimately our own, for we humans are supported by the same web of life.

Human action strengthens the planet when we move with an awareness of our interconnection with all life. Human action destroys the web when we move with the belief that we are separate, somehow immune, to the process of life on Earth. We are microcosms of the planetary condition, one body within the larger body of Mother Earth, one living realm interwoven with others in the whole of creation. This book is organized to highlight what may be called the five living realms of Mother Earth: Mineral, Plant, Animal, Human, and Oneness. Although I have separated (gently) the living body of the Earth into these realms, be aware that they function synergistically, each supporting the other, as expressed in the aspect of Oneness.

The Mineral realm includes the elements—earth, air, fire, and water—both in their Earth-shaped and human-made (for example, buildings and tools) forms. The Plant realm encompasses food crops as well as rainforests and deserts. The Animal realm includes the ones that creep and crawl, the ones that fly, the ones that swim, the domesticated as well as the wild. Many cultures and races are represented in the Human realm. Oneness is the spirit of interconnection and interdependence that bonds all aspects of creation into a related whole. The spirit of Oneness inexorably links our human kind and weaves us into the fabric of the planet.

I offer these thoughts as a backdrop against which I present images of beauty on this planet. My experience as an environmental activist taught me that people do not make fundamental changes in their attitudes toward the environment, and thus the Earth, as a result of intellectual information or campaigns based on horror or guilt. For a long time I held the belief that if only people were informed about environmental problems, they would choose automatically to change their ways. Simply knowing, however, is not enough. Knowledge must be infused with a passion for the object of one's attention, or the fire soon dies and the fervor is forgotten. Seek beauty in your life; it is a sustainable form of inspiration.

Why, you may be asking, do the images and words in this book reflect a collective "woman's view" of Mother Earth? I was weaned on collections of Ansel Adams, Eliot Porter, David Muench, and many other fine photographers, accompanied by quotes from the writings of John Muir and Henry David Thoreau and Aldo Leopold. The books truly inspired me. I reveled in the images and words. As the years passed, though, I began to notice that something was missing—where, I wondered, were the women? Surely women visited remote places and the wilds closer to home, also explored and absorbed and celebrated in words and pictures the beauty that they found. Where was the record of their journeys, the photographic footprints that marked their explorations? This book is the result of my own explorations to discover and appreciate many women's views of our planet.

The women whom I have been privileged to meet during the making of this book have shown me that many women are expressing their visions of the Earth through photography and writing. Beginning the project, I wondered whether women see and therefore photograph the world in a different way from men. I found that women are gifted with the ability to perceive and record beauty, with skill and grace, in as wide a range of styles and genres as their male colleagues. I discovered images of tenderness and power, grace and violence, intimate detail and vast breadth—the images were as diverse as the people who made them.

Although some women insist that their sex does not significantly influence *how* they photograph, almost all agree that their gender does influence how they are paid for their work. Most women report that they have experienced bias in the photographic market and received lower pay than their male counterparts. Heather Fentress comments that she used only her first initial, not her full name, when she began work as a freelance photographer because "I felt as a woman I was not taken as seriously. Maybe it was a holdover from a time when women didn't have careers, especially in the wilderness." Today, however, Heather feels that editors are looking for good *images* without regard for the photographer's gender. Despite low pay and sporadic recognition, these photographers are universally inspired about their work. Some have waited for children to grow up and leave home before single-mindedly pursuing their passion. Others have refused to wait for anything. "If women want to do something," says Pam Roberson, "they should just do it!"

Describing herself as an "Indiana Jones of the female type," Pam certainly has lived her philosophy. She thinks nothing of being airlifted into a remote area visited only once or twice a year by helicopter or biplane. "I've never really considered them wilderness areas, because there are still people around. You know, like in the Amazon, places like that. I've never been completely removed from humans." Asked if she is ever bothered by bugs, bogs, poisonous creatures, or thorny undergrowth, Pam responds, "I'm too busy thinking about the pictures I want to take. I don't have time to worry about those things. . . . Photography is intensely physical, working outdoors. I was known for my work with Arab villagers, then empty desert, then jungles and mosquito-hell tundra. It's part of knowing all the Earth; I feel globally entranced more than microscopically."

Passion buoys these women through situations that others might find intolerable. "A lot of these pictures would be *dangerous* to take," said my nephew while we were looking through some of the transparencies. After bushwhacking through Australian rainforests, sloshing through Scottish bogs, and enduring the heat of southern India, I know why few people choose to concentrate on wilderness photography. Only a special breed of human, male or female, would endure and even delight in some of the remoter parts of the planet. Many of these women have ventured into areas that would make all but the hardiest of travelers squeamish.

Their passion for beauty and adventure, however, draws them irresistibly. Nancy Webb, for example, gives her husband, Charles, a lot of credit for her photography. He has the indispensable job of poling their boat through the cypress swamps of Louisiana, where they often have to get out of the boat and drag it through shallow or weedy sections. He also watches for alligators. "Seriously, he really does," says Nancy. "I get so carried away with shooting that I don't always look where I am. Once I started to step out of the boat onto a 'log,' only to have Charles pull me back when he saw bubbles from a big gator."

Rita Summers began photographing in 1976. "I started by going along on photo trips with my husband," she explains. "I swore I would never go back to some of the hot, mosquito-infested places we went, but once I picked up a camera I was hooked and have spent weeks enjoying those same places, sitting in a stiff blind with mosquitoes swarming and sometimes even leeches swimming around my ankles. I love to work alone and often take off for a week or two in my camper." Many women echo her experience; dangers, real or imagined, mean little when pursuing a passion.

Above all, the photographers represented in this book are seekers of beauty who thrive on being close to the source of their passion. They have come to their work from a variety of backgrounds, for as many reasons as there are women. "How and why do I do what I do?" writes Pam Roberson. "Because I need the sky above me like others need money in the bank; I need it to feel good, to feel alive, alert, awake, keenly excited. I need to share those feelings with others so they pause a moment and say 'Ah.'"

Erica Wangsgard finds intense beauty in the miniature. Her eye is finely tuned to pattern and design, an outgrowth of her training as a painter. She has combined the fields of fine art and photography with her hand-colored photographic works. For her, beauty is an intimate experience, to be found in wind-brushed sand, water-sculpted rock, and freshly cooled lava.

Priscilla Connell spends as much time as she possibly can photographing. "When I'm not actively photographing, I'm probably thinking about it. Sometimes I wonder if I should be doing something else, but then I think, 'Why should I spend time doing other things when I would rather be photographing? After all,' I tell myself, 'I'm not getting any younger, and life, short as it is, should be enjoyed and lived to the fullest.' And so I plan to 'seize' the rest of my life by letting photography (that's gotten into my blood and soul) be a vital and exciting and consuming interest."

These are the effects of passion. It's the kind of energy that propels you out of bed in the morning and draws you to the window (or tent flap) to see what's happening in the world—to see, with as true an eye as you can muster, and record, with as much technical accuracy as you can attain, the ephemeral splendor of the moment. As Priscilla says, "I hope I expose the film at the right time and in the right light before the picture vanishes forever."

Not only women photographers, but also women writers, can be guides to viewing the Earth in a new way. Annie Dillard refocused my internal eye through her writings. Her book *Pilgrim at Tinker Creek* articulated many things that swam just below the surface of my awareness and spotlighted pathways where I had never ventured. She showed me how to look at the world with eyes of love, so that I might have half a chance of actually *seeing* something.

I wanted to look through other lenses as well, to explore the writings of other women, so I searched library shelves and discovered talented writers with an inspired vision of the Earth. I rejoiced in the writings of twelfth-century mystic and prophet Hildegard of Bingen, an abbess who recorded her mystical visions as well as a system of natural medicine. She painted, composed music, admonished Pope Anastasius IV (and lived to tell about it), and administered a small queendom until her death in 1179. I discovered the journal of a city-bred wife, Grace Gallatin Seton, who left her cozy Victorian home in the East to adventure across the still undisturbed mountains and plains of the West. I vicariously followed the trail of Lois Crisler, who spent more than a year filming wolves and caribou in Alaska's Brooks Range. I found native women who wrote with great eloquence—Leslie Marmon Silko, Paula Gunn Allen, and Louise Erdrich. I read and pondered and breathed the works of Anne Cameron, Susan Griffin, Cathy Johnson, Rachel Carson, Dolores LaChapelle, and many others.

Ann Zwinger led me into the desert and taught me the reality of living in a "bare bones landscape." Like the women photographers, she was willing to endure conditions that would deter all but the most devoted: "For 360 degrees I mark not a tree, not a shrub over three feet high, not a glint of water, only a light-absorbing heat-inhaling landscape that translates heat into wavering light and light into shimmering heat so that one inhales, smells, touches only heat, listens only to heat drying skin and cracking silt." In contrast, Dian Fossey, whose study of mountain gorillas required intense physical effort, guided me into a landscape with entirely different challenges. "Most people," writes Fossey, "when they think of Africa, envision dry plains sweltering under a never-ending sun. When I think of Africa I think only of the Montane rain forest of the Virungas—cold and misty, with an average annual rainfall of seventy-two inches."

These women and many other fine writers honed and polished my inner lens and challenged me to look afresh, with a finely tuned mind as well as eye and heart, at our blue and green orb gently turning through space.

We live in an extremely verbal culture, one that pays more attention to words than to actions. The traditional people of Australia's Western Desert taught me the importance of learning by watching and then experiencing. They never explained how to do something with words; they let me observe and then gently guided my fumbling hands and mind and body when I could not imitate their fluid motions. I offer these words, then, in lieu of a gentle hand to guide your perceptions, to help you see in a new way. I hope that the selected writings will sustain you when your eyes and heart are dry and dusty, when you have trouble seeing the beauty of the world around you.

I do not aim to preserve a memory of the wilderness through this book, capturing images like tigers in a zoo. A zoo is no place to meet a tiger; it is meant to roam free, without bars or gawking tourists. Likewise, a book is no place to experience the vitality of Earth. Instead, this book is meant to sharpen your vision, adjust the radar of your heart, and inspire you to look afresh at the world. You have been offered the privilege of seeing through others' eyes, of feeling through others' hearts. Go, now, and visit the tiger on her own ground. See with loving eyes. Meet the Earth on her own terms, and be renewed by the journey.

Walk in beauty.

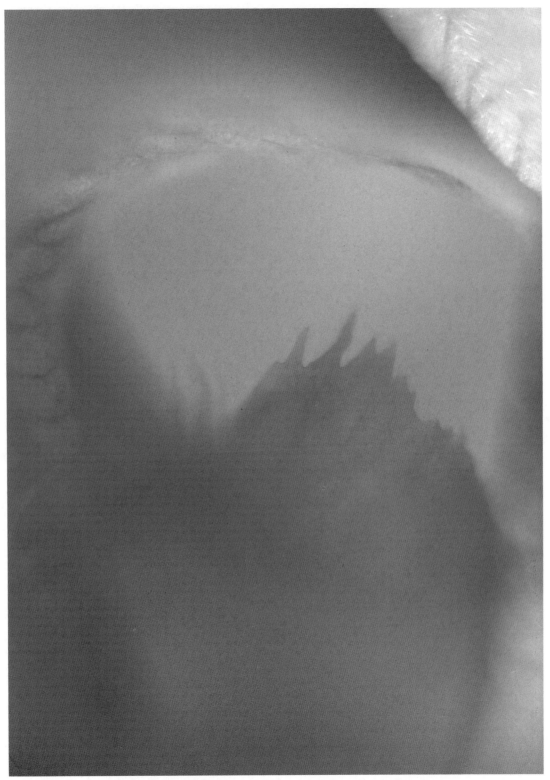

KAREN'S IRIS. HALCYON, CALIFORNIA. MARY ELLEN SCHULTZ.

SANDSTONE WALL DETAIL IN SLOT CANYON. ANTELOPE CANYON, ARIZONA. LINDE WAIDHOFER.

MINERAL REALM

A rock has being or spirit, although we may not
understand it. The spirit may differ from the spirit
we know in animals or plants or in ourselves. In
the end we all originate from the depths of the
earth. Perhaps this is how all beings share in the
spirit of the Creator.

—LESLIE MARMON SILKO
"Landscape, History, and the Pueblo Imagination"

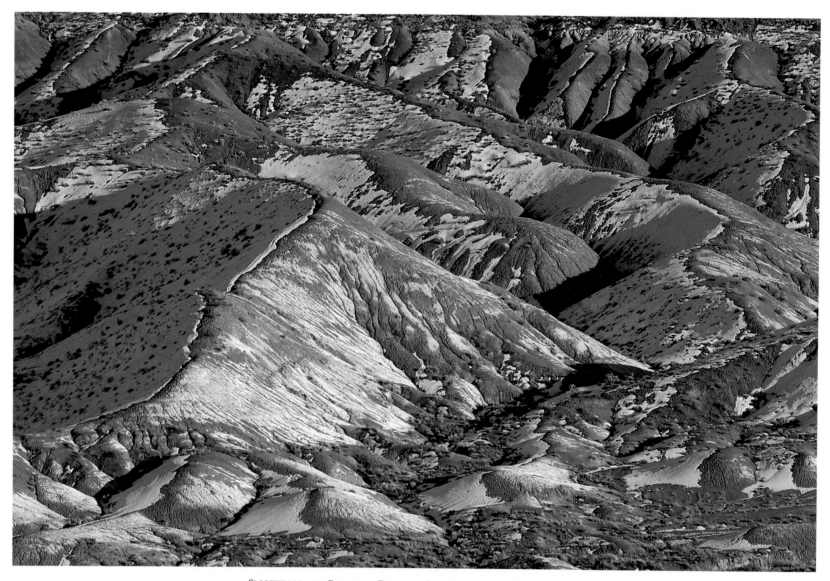

SNOWFALL ON PAINTED DESERT, ARIZONA. HEATHER ANGEL.

The mountains' bones poke through, all shoulder and knob and shin. All that summer conceals, winter reveals.

—ANNIE DILLARD
Pilgrim at Tinker Creek

Intricacy
from Pilgrim at Tinker Creek

ANNIE DILLARD

THINK OF A GLOBE, a revolving globe on a stand. Think of a contour globe, whose mountain ranges cast shadows, whose continents rise in bas-relief above the oceans. But then: think how it *really* is. These heights aren't just suggested; they're there. Pliny, who knew the world was round, figured that when it was all surveyed the earth would be seen to resemble in shape, not a sphere, but a pineapple, pricked by irregularities. When I think of walking across a continent I think of all the neighborhood hills, the tiny grades up which children drag their sleds. It is all so sculptured, three-dimensional, casting a shadow. What if you had an enormous globe in relief that was so huge it showed roads and houses—a geological survey globe, a quarter of a mile to an inch—of the whole world, and the ocean floor! Looking at it, you would know what had to be left out: the free-standing sculptural arrangement of furniture in rooms, the jumble of broken rocks in a creek bed, tools in a box, labyrinthine ocean liners, the shape of snap-dragons, walrus. Where is the one thing you care about on earth, the molding of one face? The relief globe couldn't begin to show trees, between whose overlapping boughs birds raise broods, or the furrows in bark, where whole creatures, creatures easily invisible, live out their lives and call it world enough.

What do I make of all this texture? What does it mean about the kind of world in which I have been set down? The texture of the world, its filigree and scrollwork, means that there is the possibility for beauty here, a beauty inexhaustible in its complexity, which opens to my knock, which answers in me a call I do not remember calling, and which trains me to the wild and extravagant nature of the spirit I seek.

In the eighteenth century, when educated European tourists visited the Alps, they deliberately blindfolded their eyes to shield themselves from the evidence of the earth's horrid irregularity. It is hard to say if this was not merely affectation, for today, newborn infants, who have not yet been taught our ideas of beauty, repeatedly show in tests that they prefer complex to simple designs. At any rate, after the Romantic Revolution, and after Darwin, I might add, our conscious notions of beauty changed. Were the earth as smooth as a ball bearing, it might be beautiful seen from another planet, as the rings of Saturn are. But here we live and move; we wander up and down the banks of the creek, we ride a railway through the Alps, and the landscape shifts and changes. Were the earth smooth, our brains would be smooth as well; we would wake, blink, walk two steps to get the whole picture, and lapse into a dreamless sleep. Because we are living people, and because we are on the receiving end of beauty, another element necessarily enters the question. The texture of space is a condition of time. Time is the warp and matter the weft of the woven texture of beauty in space, and death is the hurtling shuttle. Did those eighteenth-century people think they were immortal? Or were their carriages stalled to rigidity, so that they knew they would never move again, and, panicked, they reached for their blindfolds?

What I want to do, then, is add time to the texture, paint the landscape on an unrolling scroll, and set the giant relief globe spinning on its stand.

Last year I had a very unusual experience. I was awake, with my eyes closed, when I had a dream. It was a small dream about time.

I was dead, I guess, in deep black space high up among many white stars. My own consciousness had been disclosed to me, and I was happy. Then I saw far below me a long, curved band of color. As I came closer, I saw that it stretched endlessly in either direction, and I understood that I was seeing all the time of the planet where I had lived. It looked like a woman's tweed scarf; the longer I studied any one spot, the more dots of color I saw. There was no end to the deepness and variety of the dots. At length I started to look for my time, but, although more and more specks of color and deeper and more intricate textures appeared in the fabric, I couldn't find my time, or any time at all that I recognized as being near my time. I couldn't make out so much as a pyramid. Yet as I looked at the band of time, all the individual people, I understood with special clarity, were living at that very moment with great emotion, in intricate detail, in their individual times and places, one by one, like stitches in which whole worlds of feeling and energy were wrapped, in a never-ending cloth. I remembered suddenly the color and texture of our life as we knew it—these things had been utterly forgotten—and I thought as I searched for it on the limitless band, "That was a good time then, a good time to be living." And I began to remember our time.

I recalled green fields with carrots growing, one by one, in slender rows. Men and women in bright vests and scarves came and pulled the carrots out of the soil and carried them in baskets to shaded kitchens, where they scrubbed them with yellow brushes under running water. I saw white-faced cattle lowing and wading in creeks, with dust on the whorled and curly white hair between their ears. I saw May apples in forests, erupting through leaf-strewn paths. Cells on the root hairs of sycamores split and divided, and apples grew spotted and striped in the fall. Mountains kept their cool caves, and squirrels raced home to their nests through sunlight and shade.

I remembered the ocean, and I seemed to be in the ocean myself, swimming over orange crabs that looked like coral, or off the deep Atlantic banks where whitefish school. Or again I saw the tops of poplars, and the whole sky brushed with clouds in pallid streaks, under which wild ducks flew with outstretched necks, and called, one by one, and flew on.

All these things I saw. Scenes grew in depth and sunlit detail before my eyes, and were replaced by ever more scenes, as I remembered the life of my time with increasing feeling.

At last I saw the earth as a globe in space, and I recalled the ocean's shape and the form of continents, saying to myself with surprise as I looked at the planet, "Yes, that's how it was then; that part there we called. . . 'France.'" I was filled with deep affection of nostalgia—and then I opened my eyes.

We Have a Beautiful Mother

We have a beautiful
mother
Her hills
are buffaloes
Her buffaloes
hills.

We have a beautiful
mother
Her oceans
are wombs
Her wombs
oceans.

We have a beautiful
mother
Her teeth
the white stones
at the edge
of the water
the summer
grasses
her plentiful
hair.

We have a beautiful
mother
Her green lap
immense
Her brown embrace
eternal
Her blue body
everything
we know.

—ALICE WALKER
*Her Blue Body
Everything We Know*

REED POND WITH ROCKS. YELLOWSTONE NATIONAL PARK, WYOMING. JOANNE PAVIA.

FULL MOON OVER CHOLATSE. KHUMBU REGION, NEPAL. JENNY HAGER.

The Most-Sacred Mountain

Space and the twelve clean winds of heaven,
And this sharp exultation, like a cry, after the slow six thousand
    feet of climbing!
This is Tai Shan, the beautiful, the most holy.

Below my feet the foot-hills nestle, brown with flecks of green;
    and lower down the flat brown plain, the floor of earth,
    stretches away to blue infinity.

. . . .

Space, and the twelve clean winds are here;
And with them broods eternity—a swift, white peace, a presence
    manifest.

*   *   *

But I shall go down from their airy space, this swift white peace,
    this stinging exultation;
And time will close about me, and my soul stir to the rhythm
    of the daily round.
Yet, having known, life will not press so close, and always I
    shall feel time ravel thin about me;
For once I stood
In the white windy presence of eternity.

—EUNICE TIETJENS
The Home Book of Modern Verse

THE HOODOOS AT DAWN. BRYCE CANYON NATIONAL PARK, UTAH. LINDE WAIDHOFER.

I WISH I COULD sit here for eons and watch as these sandstone walls crumble, grain by grain, and fall to floor this dry wash, become rearranged by water and wind, compressed to other cliffs, excavated into other canyons, and feel the wind all the same. The rock changes, the channel changes, the wind just carries air from one place to another, more constant than the rock. The rock is ephemeral, the wind, eternal.

—ANN ZWINGER
Wind in the Rock

STORMY OCEAN. NORTH OF JENNER, CALIFORNIA, ON SONOMA COUNTY COAST. GAY BUMGARNER.

To the Taoists, water's intuitive, harmonious flow was wiser than the rational attitudes of a linear, man-over-nature mind. Thus, according to the ancient Taoist Kuan-Tzu, "the solution for the sage who would transform the world lies in water." Our present-day willfulness has taught us much about our own separate selves and little about how to live wisely and at one with the world. Only now are we recalling that there is a Tao at play in the world; and understanding its way may well help us find reunion with our own, and the earth's, body.

—BRENDA PETERSON
Living by Water

THE SECRET OF SEEING is, then, the pearl of great price. If I thought he could teach me to find it and keep it forever I would stagger barefoot across a hundred deserts after any lunatic at all. But although the pearl may be found, it may not be sought. The literature of illumination reveals this above all: although it comes to those who wait for it, it is always, even to the more practiced and adept, a gift and a total surprise.

—ANNIE DILLARD
Pilgrim at Tinker Creek

Rowboat reflected in Rudd Pond. Becket, Massachusetts. Annie Tiberio.

THE BRILLIANT WHITE of an iceberg lies on a thick, wide base of blue that might be as ancient as the earth. The icebergs take all shapes, and some have fissures through which a searing blue light shines. . . . [we] drift along the peninsula, through an ice-sculpture garden. Herodotus said you never step in the same stream twice. The Antarctic version of that is never seeing the same iceberg twice. Because the icebergs are always changing, one sees a unique and personal iceberg, which no one else has ever seen or ever will see.

—DIANE ACKERMAN
The New Yorker Magazine

ICEBERG. ANVERS ISLAND, ANTARCTICA. SHARON CHESTER.

MARSH MARIGOLDS BY GREEN FALLS. GUNNISON NATIONAL FOREST, COLO. BRENDA THARP.

THERE IS NOTHING in nature that can't be taken as a sign of both mortality and invigoration. Cascading water equates loss followed by loss, a momentum of things falling in the direction of death, then life. . . . Water can stand for what is unconscious, restorative and sexual in us, for the creative swill in which we fish for our ideas. It carries, weightlessly, the imponderable things in our lives: death and creation. We can drown in it or else stay buoyant, quench our thirst, stay alive.

—GRETEL EHRLICH
The Solace of Open Spaces

T HE SEA DOES NOT reward those who are too anxious, too greedy, or too impatient. To dig for treasures shows not only impatience and greed, but lack of faith. Patience, patience, patience, is what the sea teaches. Patience and faith. One should lie empty, open, choiceless as a beach—waiting for a gift from the sea.

—ANNE MORROW LINDBERGH
Gift from the Sea

SAND WORM CASTING. CAPE HILLSBORO NATIONAL PARK, AUSTRALIA. JUDITH BOICE.

P UEBLO POTTERS, the creators of petroglyphs and oral narratives, never conceived of removing themselves from the earth and sky. So long as the human consciousness remains *within* the hills, canyons, cliffs, and the plants, clouds, and sky, the term *landscape,* as it has entered the English language, is misleading. "A portion of territory the eye can comprehend in a single view" does not correctly describe the relationship between the human being and his or her surroundings. This assumes the viewer is somehow *outside* or *separate from* the territory he or she surveys. Viewers are as much a part of the landscape as the boulders they stand on. There is no high mesa edge or mountain peak where one can stand and not immediately be part of all that surrounds.

—LESLIE MARMON SILKO
"Landscape, History, and the Pueblo Imagination"

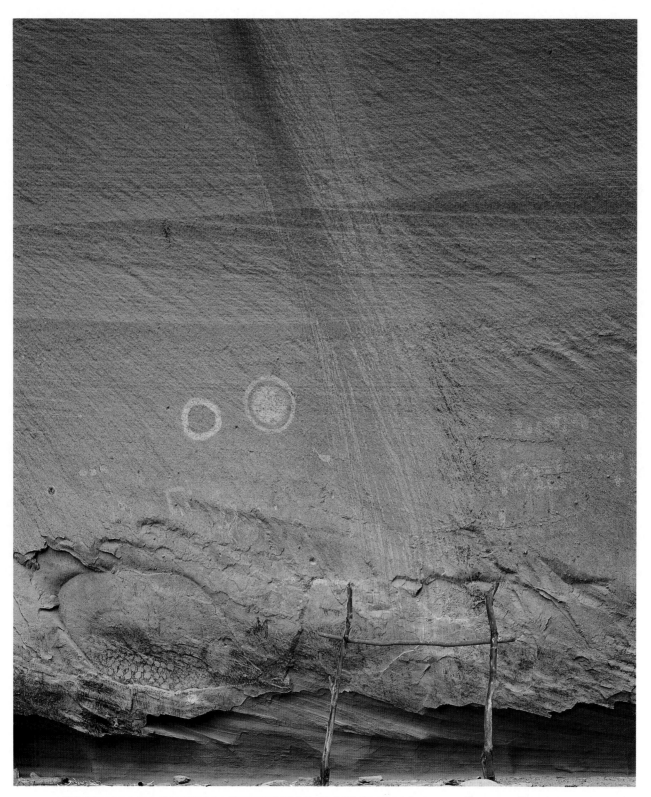

WEAVING LOOM, CANYON DE CHELLY NATIONAL MONUMENT, ARIZONA. BARBARA BRUNDEGE.

DUNESCAPE. GREAT SAND DUNES NATIONAL PARK, COLORADO. PAM ROBERSON.

I HAD NO READING of magnitude when I first saw [the dunes] from the air, no sense of scale. They might as well have been ripples on a beach. But on the ground, this floating evening, the dunes are impressive and massive, unforgettable. Wherever I trace a horizon, I follow an elegant line that protects and defines, brings order and serenity into a chaotic world.

—ANN ZWINGER
The Mysterious Lands

CANDY-STRIPED SANDSTONE. JURASSIC SANDSTONE, COLORADO PLATEAU. LINDE WAIDHOFER.

A ND SOMETIMES there is nothing at all in the desert's ultimate economy of means—obstacles removed, trees dispensed with, objects discarded along the way, just to get down to this precise, bare bones landscape.

—ANN ZWINGER
The Mysterious Lands

T HE SHADOW'S THE THING. Outside shadows are blue, I read, because they are lighted by the blue sky and not the yellow sun. Their blueness bespeaks infinitesimal particles scattered down infinitesimal distance. Muslims, whose religion bans representational art as idolatrous, don't observe the rule strictly; but they do forbid sculpture, because it casts a shadow. So shadows define the real. . . . They inform my eyes of my location here, here O Israel, here in the world's flawed sculpture, here in the flickering shade of the nothingness between me and the light.

—ANNIE DILLARD
Pilgrim at Tinker Creek

ARTILLERY ROCK NEAR MELBOURNE, AUSTRALIA. OIL PAINT ON PHOTOGRAPHIC LINEN. ERICA WANGSGARD.

On the feast day of Mary the fragrant,
Mother of the shepherd of the flocks,
I cut a handful of the new corn,
I dried it gently in the sun,
I rubbed it sharply from the husk,
With my own palms.
I ground it in a quern on Friday,
I baked it on a fan of sheepskin,
I toasted it to a fire of rowan,
And I shared it round my people.
I went sunways round my dwelling
In name of the Mary Mother.

—GAELIC ISLES OF SCOTLAND

GODDESS SHEELA-NA-GIG, NUNNERY RUINS, ISLE OF IONA, SCOTLAND. JUDITH BOICE.

AERIAL CLOUDS OVER INDONESIA. KATHLEEN THORMOD CARR.

THROUGHOUT TIME and place, people have been obsessed with the many moods of the sky. Not just because their crops and journeys depended on the weather, but because the sky is such a powerful symbol. The sky that gods inhabit, the sky whose permanence we depend on and take for granted, as if it really were a solid, vaulted ceiling on which stars were painted, as our ancestors thought. . . . We picture the sky as the final resting place of those we love, as if their souls were perfumed aerosol. We bury them among pine needles and worms, but in our imaginations we give them a lighter-than-air journey into some recess of the sky from which they will watch over us. "High" is where lofty sentiments dwell, where the "high and mighty" live, where choirs of angels sing. I don't know why the sky symbolizes our finest ideals and motives, unless, lacking in self-confidence, we think our acts of mercy, generosity, and heroism are not intrinsic qualities, not characteristics human beings alone can muster, but temporary gifts from some otherworldly power situated in the sky. Stymied by events, or appalled by human nature, we sometimes roll our eyes upward, to where we believe our fate is dished out in the mansions of the stars.

—DIANE ACKERMAN
A Natural History of the Senses

I F THE LANDSCAPE reveals one certainty, it is that the extravagant gesture is the very stuff of creation. After the one extravagant gesture of creation in the first place, the universe has continued to deal exclusively in extravagances, flinging intricacies and colossi down aeons of emptiness, heaping profusions on profligacies with ever-fresh vigor. The whole show has been on fire from the word go. I come down to the water to cool my eyes. But everywhere I look I see fire; that which isn't flint is tinder, and the whole world sparks and flames.

—ANNIE DILLARD
Pilgrim at Tinker Creek

LAVA FLOWING INTO SEA AT NIGHT. ISLAND OF HAWAII. KATHLEEN THORMOD CARR.

M ANY OF US NEED this wilderness as a place to listen to the quiet, to feel at home with ancient rhythms that are absent in city life, to know the pulse of a river, the riffle of the wind, the rataplan of rain on the slickrock. Romantics, perhaps, but realists too: here in the wilderness is a safety valve for our civilization, an environment which can absorb our pollution, and, given time, cleanse itself. . . .

And what of the designated wilderness land that we still have: how does it remain wilderness? Idealistically I would like to hope that people could be educated to carry out their trash, leave no sign of their passage, disturb no prehistoric sites, knowing in this way they will come away richer. But even education and understanding will not check the wear and tear of too many people, no matter how well intentioned. The greatest danger may be in loving it to death.

—ANN ZWINGER
Wind in the Rock

CHAIR MOUNTAIN REFLECTED IN LILY LAKE AT SUNRISE. ELK MOUNTAINS, NEAR MARBLE, COLORADO. BRENDA THARP.

WILSON PEAK WITH DANDELIONS. SAN JUAN MOUNTAINS, COLORADO. LINDE WAIDHOFER.

PLANT REALM

We use the word "wilderness," but perhaps we mean wildness. Isn't that why I've come here? In wilderness, I seek the wildness in myself—and in so doing, come on the wildness everywhere around me because, after all, being part of nature, I'm cut from the same cloth.

—GRETEL EHRLICH
"River History"

SKUNK CABBAGE AND BERRY VINE. WALTON, NEW YORK. BARBARA BRUNDEGE.

THE EARTH'S VEGETATION is part of a web of life in which there are intimate and essential relations between plants and the earth, between plants and other plants, between plants and animals. Sometimes we have no choice but to disturb these relationships, but we should do so thoughtfully, with full awareness that what we do may have consequences remote in time and place.

—RACHEL CARSON
Silent Spring

The Old Cherry Tree

from Brief Cherishing: A Napa Valley Harvest

HILDEGARD FLANNER

TOGETHER WITH A FEW human beings, dead and living, and their achievements, trees are what I most love and revere. In my life and my concerns I have defended trees that are threatened and praised them when they are ignored; for their sakes I have made enemies of friends and neighbors. The knowledge that in a western canyon I am the owner of very tall straight redwoods and firs gives me pride of citizenship beyond anything I might accomplish by my own efforts. I have taken a serious kind of joy and a delightful kind of peace in their shade, and at night I have watched the shaggy white planets pass above their dark branches. I have loved trees, I have planted trees and have been excited to grow a tree from seed and discover the first minute signs of unfolding life that will, some distant year, become a rooted tower or a spreading bower of rustling foliage. I am fortunate to live where native trees are numerous and where horticulture is popular and every rural family has an orchard.

Our own orchard is old and contains many trees that are dilapidated, but even the most dilapidated have been safe for years because each time I look at them, aware of their crookedness and awkward appearance, I also see some odd curve of bough or improvisation of flowering that makes sudden poetry of them and of their trashiness. They are thus protected, although they should, under good management, be sensibly discarded and replaced. Yet the more dubious they look the more they resemble the paintings of Oriental masters and suggest the fresh enduring emotions of the ancient anthologies. Perhaps there is universal truth in implying that real meaning is wrung out at the last moment, and the last moment must be prolonged. Whose duty is that? Really not mine. Yet I have discerned it. I am involved in its total meaning, of tree and of human. Still, as I myself grow older and, alas, much older, the image of new young trees in place of the old ones creeps temptingly into my mind. It is a troubling image and its disturbance, just now, settles on the spirit of a woman wandering and trying to think in an old orchard.

If I could have the sense and courage to take down a decrepit tree in spite of its fanatical habit of reminding me of the brave words of General Su Wu written down 2,000 years ago as he sadly embraced his wife for the last time, and in spite of its mad annual impulse to bloom and bear and spill bushels of amethyst prunes and rosy apples on the ground, it might be for me a spiritual rejuvenation and consequently even a beneficial thing for the flesh as well. But conscience is tyrannical. It is a womanly vice. I have become the guardian not of my own but of whatever other life remains in the earth I possess. It is hard to be wise and natural. Although my husband is no longer living I can guess what he might wish to do. To remove a tree that had lasted too long and replace it might well please him. This thought is a poignant incentive, also a consolation for the choice I foresee as melancholy and difficult, whenever it must be made.

The decision I am afraid of on a mild February morning of our western spring, is one for advice from a clinical priest. It is beyond horticulture. It becomes moral. In my mind it faces and fights itself and I am torn. Must I continue to identify myself with the aged, no longer serviceable and eccentric trees, or do I dare to relate myself to young trees with futures, good looks and green chances of tonic sap? My orchard, by usual standards, is conspicuously shabby. This hurts me. And as I look around I notice a few unrewarding cherry trees.

To get a cherry in our orchard has meant to rise early, before birds or worms are awake, and snatch at a fruit or two as day breaks. One summer, in order to enjoy the large luscious black Bings, my husband ordered a nylon net he saw advertised in an agricultural supply magazine. The advertisement promised protection to fruit from marauding birds and complete accessibility for the picker. If all of this was true, we were not the ones to demonstrate it. As we hoisted the net on poles to the top of the tree the clinging mesh snagged every twig on the way up; then, as we squinted into the sun and gave helpful and confusing suggestions to each other on how to free the net to slide down as directed, we found that it could descend only by being profanely and scrupulously removed from twig to clutching twig. However, the picture as given of happy people congratulating each other outside the net while the cherries waxed abnormally big and the birds fretted on the next tree—in the advertisement they were scowling—this fine fiction was worth keeping in mind until suddenly and utterly we tied ourselves in. The next step was just to ripen along with the cherries in boredom and frustration, while the birds jeered nastily. This very personal recollection comes back to me as I find myself standing under a cherry tree, not the one that lassoed us, but a very old pie-cherry tree, largest and surely the oldest inhabitant of the orchard. Indeed, where is there in the entire valley a cherry tree so old and so big? It is a tree known in the neighborhood, and when we first came here to live friendly strangers drove up our hill and requested, "Just a few cherries, please, from the old tree, enough for the wife to make one pie."

Now so much of the tree is fallen or dead that there is scarcely enough fruit for a robin to make one cherry tart. I get none myself, even on tiptoe or a ladder. And the trifle of birdsong it holds is nothing to give regard to. Neither has it grown ancient with picturesque aspects. All of its gifts are gone. Even the child with a little basket passes by. It is too large, you see, to be forgotten, yet neglect is its fate today. And so I talk to myself as I look up and see no buds swelling toward wide-open blossoms where the bees should soon be rolling. From something so unpromising, what is to be expected? Why is it so difficult for me to say, "It is time, old cherry tree"?

This happens to be the day on which my son is preparing a level space where there will be built a storehouse of tools and equipment. I welcome this plan as one to maintain order. Not only his powerful tractor, but various archaic automobiles considered by him too beautiful and valuable to go to the dump, can now be respectably housed, particularly that very sacred hot-chili-red truck that usurps the sight of grace and elegance where my tallest bamboo has established its feather culms. This is a day of orchard and premises keeping and its purposes begin to take hold of me. I look up at the cherry and assess what I see. Crippled and lumpy, here and there split, beheaded of several heads, and to all appearances so nearly dead that there seems no way to say it is alive. Then I look up at the sky and straighten, as if to think of other things. A good clear morning to be alive myself. And John has opened the deer gate and is driving the loud clanging tractor into the orchard toward the work that makes ready for his storehouse.

"Oh, John," I call. He doesn't hear above the roar of the machine. Without thinking I reach out and touch the subject I was about to speak of. I touch not only a tree of bark and wood but with tingling certainty in my fingers I touch an entire century. At this spot there stood a house which no longer exists. The spring that served its occupants still serves us from its cold stone trough at the edge of the nearby woods. And a county clerk had written the first deed to this property, dated 1878, in script almost too lace-like to read or believe. It was then that the tree was planted and began to work for men and birds and until this spring it has never stopped working. It was always the first to bloom and ripen, always prompt no matter that the weather might delay, still it brought on its sweet sparkling globes of fruit. For 100 years of faithfulness there should be a reward. Hang the old tree with garlands, strike up the fiddle. But I am caught up in another momentum. Again I call, "Oh, John!" He can't hear, there is too much noise. I go closer. "Maybe it's time," I shout, and he yells, "What is it?" How hard it is now for me to be positive and loud, quick and wise. But I must not take time to be careful. I am committed. "Time to take down the old cherry tree," I shriek.

I know that decisions like this should be made in quietness and deliberately. We should live slowly, even timidly, in imagination with all the possible results of the irrevocable. Once down, there would never be an up to this deed. I exercise a frightening power. It is not exactly a choice between life and death because life is already attacked by mean and obvious details of the end. However, the power of termination is awesome. Naturally, it chokes me. I cough. Kings, tyrants, judges—how have they arrived at that last fatal word that condemns life without feeling their own lives threatened, shredded and about to come apart? But don't be silly, I say to myself. What are you talking about? Just get on with what there is to do. Isn't this the mistake you have always been making? Too much emphasis on the wrong thing while you let the right thing drift? "John!" I shriek again. "Time to take down the old cherry tree!"

"Yes, yes," he says easily, "I can hear you," and I become aware that he has turned off the noise of the tractor and also that in the interval of silence I can hear the demented sound of the ranging peacock that forages in the foothills and ravines near our place. It always seems to be a sound of mental stress and at this moment it is right for my state of mind.

I am surprised by hesitation on John's part. "I don't think I can cut it down, it's too big," he says. "I'll have to push it down." Again he seems doubtful. "If I can."

And the tractor starts again. Then for a while he is busy with his work of leveling nearby, but as I stand watching he begins to look at the old cherry tree in a calculating way. I suspect that he welcomes my decision to get rid of a tree so dominant yet unproductive in this place, and he must be astonished. He circles and comes closer. I cringe and brace myself for the shock to my nerves and my conscience. John backs his tractor and then goes forward with an awful clang. He hits the old cherry with a loud dull crash. It does not budge. It does not even quiver. He backs away. Again he charges forward and collides with the tree. It stands without shaking. It is only I who grow weak. I shake and feel sick. Perhaps I am wrong to condemn a creature so full of strength in spite of the many signs of being done with strength. Again the tractor charges and without effect. I would prefer to leave now, to go back to the house and hide behind closed doors where I could neither see nor hear; but it was I who started this turmoil and I must remain to see it through.

At this moment my 13-year-old grandson, Danny, arrives and stands near me, watching. "Your father is wasting a lot of good gas," I scream. "Diesel," he screams in return. "Fuel," I scream back at him, as the attack continues. Backing and charging, backing and colliding, the tractor roars and hits, and at last the old cherry tree begins to tremble. But it stands. I suffer and watch in a nauseating agony of indecision. Should I save the body while some secret obstinacy still holds it up? Or is it better to let the savage shocks continue? Suddenly John begins a new maneuver. He backs, then closes into the attack at an angle, tilts the sharp, wide blade of the tractor and digs it into the earth. Again he does this, and again, until the action of the bellowing machine and the chaos and the frightful uproar become a kind of violent choreography. I stand riveted and overcome by what I have started in the quiet orchard. Finally the tilted blade snags on a massive root. The root holds.

The contest goes on. My son will not give up. The old tree will not give up. The tractor will not give up. The boy and I stand and wait and the diabolic ballet goes on and on. The tractor, although a monolith, has been converted into a maniac of circling and twisting power. In its fierceness it is serpentine. At last, at last! With a heavy snap, a sound of fatal resignation, the root breaks. And the tree still stands! The tractor attacks it for the final time. And when the old cherry tree falls there goes down with it a century of hopes and many kinds of weather, sun and drought, of good rain and poor rain, of good pies and poor pies, and 100 years of countless round white flowers opening and coming apart and drifting down while early-rising and late-loitering birds and bees came and went and always, at the right cloistered moment there was the invisible sap slowly storming up through the trunk and into the tips of the branches, just as it was rising in a million other trees at the eternal hour given for ascensions.

While I stand and have no voice to speak, John nonchalantly gets down from his tractor and walks over to the fallen tree. He begins to peel off patches of thick bark. "Termites," he says. I do not want to see them. "More termites," he announces. I hate the sight of them. I stay where I am. Then he pulls off another, larger patch of bark. "Look here!" he cries. There is a company of small lizards, eight in all, spending the winter in the shelter of the cherry tree. John collects them and quickly puts them all down Danny's back. The boy rolls his eyes and draws up his shoulders but does not flinch.

I retrieve the young saurians and put them in the grass. Then I go to the prostrate tree to hunt for more, as if this intimacy with small creatures might reduce the magnitude of the old giant's final resignation. There seem to be no more lizards, but I find neat necklaces of empty holes, the precise work of woodpeckers whose echoing labors I have often heard. Then John, in the cavity left nearby, finds a beautiful little snake of a dark rich skin, a young gopher snake whose presence close to the tree appears to indicate dependence and community. John holds the snake for a moment and we watch as it flashes its rapid tongue in the sunlight. Then he puts it down and we see it take off, small and solitary. We are left alone with the fallen tree. It is stripped of everything, except its misshapen size, and its weighty bulk so lately upright and adamant. There it lies.

John gets his power-saw and starts methodically cutting branches for firewood. So soon does the drama and ordeal of destruction become the routine of plain use. Dazedly I pick up a few small logs. "Are you out of wood at your house?" he inquires.

"No," I answer, "this is ritual. I want a few pieces of the old cherry for my bedroom fireplace."

He tells me, "It won't burn yet. It has too much sap."

"Too much sap!" I exclaim and hastily drop the wood. "Is it still alive?"

"Well, what do you think? You saw how the old girl fought back."

His personification of the old tree horrifies me and I begin to cry.

John gives me a well-controlled look. "You're queer," he comments.

With difficulty I inquire, "What's the diameter?"

"Three feet at least, I guess. Big for an orchard tree." And he goes to work again.

In wretchedness I pick up the pieces of wood and hug them, small logs of smooth bark ornamented with delicate silver-green medallions of lichen. I carry them ashamedly to my bedroom porch. When I lay them down I know that I will never burn them, ever, no matter how long I keep them to lose their sap. They are too elegant, they have too much meaning. I shall never wish to warm myself at their melancholy and accusing blaze.

I return to the orchard. It is a still, empty place now. John has driven his tractor back through the deer gate and Danny has gone with him. I stand and stare at the remains of the old cherry, the limbs in a heap, thick bark strewn, the powerful roots split and twisted. Now no one else will know if I give in to tears as I realize that there must always be new questions in my mind about the imperfection of my decision to remove the old tree. I have learned, too late, that there is more to life than what is visible. The greater strength had been underground and out of sight, and I had grossly, stupidly, not even guessed it was there. You fool, you made a wrong choice and you only proved that decisions are hell, a fact you've known since tormented childhood when it was not possible to be sure whether vanilla or strawberry or chocolate was the right choice, or whether to wear the sash with rosebuds woven into the silk or the blue satin one or the one with Roman stripes. I observe how tough the roots are and how strong and sharp and that they point up with a kind of spiraling hiss into the placid noon sky. How dreadfully eloquent they look, expressing all that I felt for them. It is not easy to stand alone with them.

Something prods me into an attempt to understand that the moment holds a finality beyond agitation. In weariness I can only decide that an urban-minded person would take this with helpful sanity, and I shall never be an urban-minded person. "For you they pulled out oak, fir, madrone and manzanita," I say to the roots. "It was a long time ago. Do you remember?"

For many minutes I stand here where the first axe wound and the first gouge of the plowshare cut into this very ground at my feet where the old cherry tree has just been knocked over. Now I hear the tractor again. It is down in the vineyard. "All right," I say, "it's true that I am queer. I talk to trees. I talk to roots. It's true they can't answer. But they have a lot to say. Look at them!" And I myself look at the roots where they lie on top of their trash, full of fierce power in every slashed point that thrusts up, full of a cherry tree voice, full of a forest voice, the forest that fell to make room for an orchard 100 years ago.

I start back to the house. "Just to get out of earshot," I tell myself.

IT WAS ARCHITECT Mies van der Rohe who said, "God dwells in the details." Scientists study fractals to find the order hidden within chaos, the details of our world. Fractals—those things that reveal ever more detail as they are subjected to magnification; we are discovering that they suggest an underlying order in things as diverse as stock market fluctuations, flooding, evolutionary leaps, animal behavior, and the order hidden within the chaos of a running stream. I catch hints and whispers of a beneficent universe. . . . Our familiar, intimate environment is a universe in itself—and one full of delightful revelations.

—CATHY JOHNSON

On Becoming Lost: A Naturalist's Search for Meaning

PALM LEAVES. KONA, HAWAII. JENNY HAGER.

GLACIER LILIES. TETON NATIONAL PARK, WYOMING. LINDE WAIDHOFER.

Does anything eat flowers? I couldn't recall ever having seen anything actually eat a flower—are they nature's privileged pets?

—ANNIE DILLARD
Pilgrim at Tinker Creek

SPRING BEAUTY AND DWARF CLOVER. MOUNT EVANS, COLORADO. LINDE WAIDHOFER.

THERE IS AN ART to wandering. If I have a destination, a plan—an objective—I've lost the ability to find serendipity. I've become too focused, too single-minded. I am on a quest, not a ramble. I search for the Holy Grail of particularity and miss the chalice freely offered, filled full and overflowing.

—CATHY JOHNSON
On Becoming Lost: A Naturalist's Search for Meaning

. . . it is only framed in space that beauty blooms. Only in space are events and objects and people unique and significant—and therefore beautiful. A tree has significance if one sees it against the empty face of sky. A note in music gains significance from the silence on either side. A candle flowers in the space of night. Even small and casual things take on significance if they are washed in space, like a few autumn grasses in one corner of an Oriental painting, the rest of the page bare.

—ANNE MORROW LINDBERGH
Gift from the Sea

RAVEN TRACKS AT PINE CREEK. ZION NATIONAL PARK, UTAH. BARBARA BRUNDEGE.

EARTH STAR DISPERSING SPORES. HEATHER ANGEL.

OLD [EARTHSTARS] GAVE OFF a cloud of spores when I touched their globular centers; a little hole in the top spouted out a small cloud of dust whenever the round part was pressed, like the bulb of a syringe. Others still were firm and did not open.

It was easy to see how superstitious folk in the past could interpret strange meanings in these curious creations of the wild, how the fantasy of their forms might be related to some satanic source. Some said that earthstars were used as ingredients in witches' brews and medicines, but no one knew very much about them or cared. It was left to the botanist and mycologist to understand them, and to the artist and philosopher to appreciate their strange beauty.

—VIRGINIA S. EIFERT
Land of the Snowshoe Hare

The Mysteries (Part VI)

The mysteries remain,
I keep the same
cycle of seed-time
and of sun and rain;
Demeter in the grass,
I multiply,
renew and bless
Iacchus in the vine;
I hold the law,
I keep the mysteries true,
the first of these
to name the living dead;
I am red wine and bread.

> I KEEP THE LAW,
> I HOLD THE MYSTERIES TRUE,
> I AM THE VINE,
> THE BRANCHES, YOU
> AND YOU.

—HILDA DOOLITTLE
Collected Poems 1912–1944

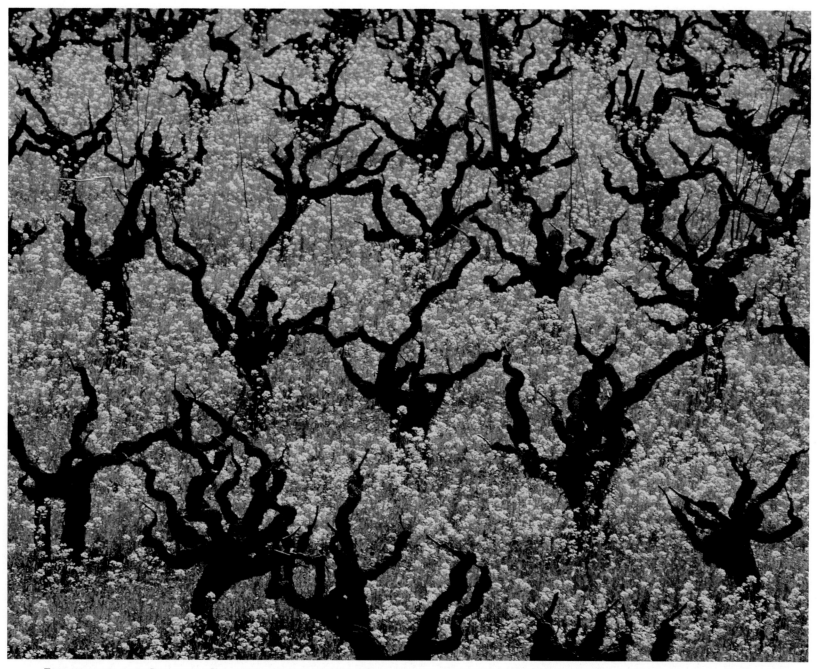

EIGHTY-YEAR-OLD CABERNET SAUVIGNON VINES AND MUSTARD WEEDS. ALEXANDER VALLEY, CALIFORNIA. KATHLEEN NORRIS COOK.

NOW ARE COME the days of brown leaves. They fall from the trees; they flutter on the ground. When the brown leaves flutter, they are saying little things. They talk with the wind. I hear them tell of their borning days, when they did come into the world as leaves. . . . Today [the leaves] were talking of the time before their borning days of this springtime. They talked on and on, and I did listen on to what they were telling the wind and the earth in their whisperings. They told how they were a part of earth and air, before their tree-borning days. And now they are going back. In gray days of winter, they go back to the earth again. But they do not die.

—OPAL WHITELEY
The Singing Creek Where the Willows Grow

FALL COLOR. ZION NATIONAL PARK, UTAH. BARBARA BRUNDEGE.

I am the one whose praise echoes on high
I adorn all the earth
I am the breeze that nurtures all things green
I encourage blossoms to flourish with ripening fruits.
I am led by the spirit to feed the purest streams.
I am the rain coming from the dew
that causes the grasses to laugh with the joy of life.
I am the yearning for good.

—HILDEGARD OF BINGEN
Meditations of Bingen

TALL PURPLE FLEABANE IN MOUNTAIN MEADOW. TROUT LAKE AND THE WILSONS, SAN JUAN MOUNTAINS, COLORADO. LINDE WAIDHOFER.

KESTREL. LORNA STANTON/ABPL.

ANIMAL REALM

If only I could live and so serve the world that after
me there should never again be birds in cages.

—ISAK DINESON (BARONESS KAREN BLIXEN)
"The Deluge at Norderney"

SANDHILL CRANES IN SUNRISE FOG. NEAR MONTE VISTA, COLORADO. WENDY SHATTIL.

I, the fiery life of divine essence, am aflame beyond the beauty of the meadows, I gleam in the waters, and I burn in the sun, moon, and stars. . . . I awaken everything to life.
—HILDEGARD OF BINGEN
Hildegard of Bingen's Book of Divine Works

Orca's Child
from Dzelarhons

ANNE CAMERON

Long ago Orca was only one colour, black, and she lived like all the other sea mammals, living in the water, coming to the surface to breathe.

Sometimes, she would lie on top of the chuck and watch Eagle Flies High riding the wind.

Eagle Flies High isn't any bigger than any other eagle, but she is strong, and she flies higher and farther, for longer periods of time, and she giggles and laughs at the things she sees below her.

Orca began to wonder what it would be like to fly in the air instead of swimming in the chuck. She watched Eagle Flies High swoop to the surface of the sea and rise back up again with Salmon caught in her strong feet, and Orca began to feel that Eagle Flies High was her special friend.

When Orca saw Eagle Flies High approaching, Orca would dive down to where Salmon lives, and she would chase Salmon up to the surface so Eagle Flies High could catch her food easily.

When Eagle Flies High realized what Orca was doing, she'd swoop over the waves, calling a thank you, telling of the things Orca would never experience, of snow high on the mountains, of small flowers in the meadows, of bushes thick with berries and of sunlight slanting through the columns of the forest.

Orca told Eagle Flies High that she had never seen a flower, and Eagle Flies High brought a foxglove and dropped it to her. Another time she brought Lupin, another time Dogwood, and when the berries were ripe, Eagle Flies High brought some for Orca to try.

Orca and Eagle Flies High became very good friends, and their friendship grew until they loved each other so strongly it was as if light came from their bodies when they saw each other.

But one was a creature of the air, and one was a creature of the sea, and neither could live in the world of the other.

Still, they loved each other, and love has a way of making sure it gets shown and expressed. Orca wanted so badly to know what it felt like to fly, fly as her love did, that she began to jump high out of the water, until there was no other creature in the sea who could jump so high.

And Eagle Flies High spent more and more of her time closer and closer to the surface of the waves, that she might be close to her love.

And one day, as Eagle Flies High swooped towards the waves, Orca leaped into the air and for one moment, their bodies touched, and their love was shown.

When their child was born, she was black like Orca, but with white on her body, like the head and tail of Eagle Flies High, and she could make piping sounds like the bird did, and she giggled.

Orca loved her baby and taught it everything a whale child should know, and Eagle Flies High tried to teach her to fly. But the new baby, though she could leap higher and farther than her mother, and spent much more time out of the sea than any other creature, could not learn to fly.

Still, the black and white baby loved to leap and jump, to giggle and sing, and to play games of every sort. No other whale enjoys life quite as much as Orca, and every new Orca baby that's born has white patches, and they're different on every new whale, no two the same.

And because these wonderful creatures are the result of love between creatures of different worlds, they are capable of love for all things.

There is a place on the west coast of Vancouver Island where the rocks stick way out into the sea, and in the old days, the women would go out there at certain times of the year, in the spring and in the fall, when Orca is moving up and down the coast.

The women would sit on the rocks and play their flutes and whistles.

Orca does not hear only with her ears, as we do. Every inch of skin on Orca's body picks up sound vibrations, and she not only hears the music, she feels it as well.

And when Orca heard and felt the music of the women, she would swim to the place where the rocks stick far out into the chuck, and she would rise up, up, up, out of the waves, until she was balanced only by her mighty tail flukes, and, with most of her body exposed to the sight of the women, she would sway to the music.

Then the women would hear the most beautiful of sounds, a sound so wonderful there are no words to describe it, a sound so full of love and truth it brought tears to the eyes, tears of happiness. The sound of Orca singing.

And the women would listen to Orca, as Orca had listened to the flutes and whistles, and sometimes, for a magical moment, the women would play their flutes as Orca sang, and the music of two different realities would blend and merge, and all creation would listen. It is said that at these times Osprey would fly up, up, up, her patterned underside exposed to view, and she would add her song to the chorus, and three realities would be joined in speech. And when this happened, the very rocks of the earth would begin to vibrate, and hum, until all of creation, for a brief moment, was united.

Then, with a final sound, Orca would splash back into the water to continue her voyage. And anyone splashed by a whale has luck, and will have happiness, for this is one of the blessings of Orca, whose very body bears the marks of a love that found its expression and blended two very different realities.

MACAQUE MOTHER AND CHILD. SHIGA HEIGHTS, JAPAN. HEATHER ANGEL.

Love is a fruit in season at all times, and within reach of every hand. Anyone may gather it and no limit is set.

—MOTHER TERESA

BLACK SKIMMER CHICKS IN NEST WITH EGG HATCHING. GULF ISLANDS NATIONAL SEASHORE, MISSISSIPPI. CONNIE TOOPS.

W HEN I GO UNPROGRAMMED, "eyes only" and open to experience, the world expands as if taking a deep breath. There is more to see—or perhaps I am able now to see it. It is a Zen-like openness, a meditative awareness. I can accept everything—or very nearly—because I am willing to. I can see what is just beyond my peripheral vision.

—CATHY JOHNSON
On Becoming Lost: A Naturalist's Search for Meaning

ROCKHOPPER PENGUINS. NEW ISLAND, WEST FALKLANDS. SHARON CHESTER.

WHY DO PEOPLE respond so strongly to penguins? First, they stand straight and walk upright, like us, so we see them as little humanoids—a convention of headwaiters, ten thousand nuns, plump babies in snowsuits. On land, they have a comical waddling walk, very similar to a human toddler's. They tend to walk right up to you: looking down, you find an affectionate creature standing as tall and straight as a young child and perhaps offering you its flipper as if to shake hands. Another reason adult penguins are easy to anthropomorphize is that they sometimes seem so much a caricature of human beings. They like company but also bicker with their neighbors; they give their mates gifts of pretty stones but also quarrel with them from time to time, have affairs, and divorce and remarry; they're affectionate, attentive parents and share the child rearing; they live in colonies that function like cities; they're plagued by adolescent gangs; they're forever waddling around at high speed, as if on important errands. They are creatures of instinct, but then so are we. Our instincts dwell under layers of inhibitions, social codes, bridled emotions, feats of mental dressage, and hand-me-down wisdom, but when it comes to the basics of hunger, sex, and child rearing they're as strong as any penguin's.

—DIANE ACKERMAN
The New Yorker Magazine

ONLY NOW after half a lifetime of observation, do I feel confident of what I have learned about beavers, and keenly aware of how much there is yet to be learned. Having no scientific training I have had to rely on common sense and perception and faithful daily observation. These have led me to disagree with those who believe that the intelligence of animals is proportional to the size of the brain, and to distrust much else of what I have read. The new science of ethology—"scientific study of animal behavior and formation of characteristics"—offers hope for the future. But only if it is pursued with love for the subject of study. There can be no understanding without love.

—DOROTHY RICHARDS WITH HOPE SAWYER BUYUKMIHCI
Beaversprite: My Years Building an Animal Sanctuary

BEAVER ON LOG IN NORBERG LAKE, BEARHEAD LAKE STATE PARK, MINNESOTA. MARTHA L. DAVIS.

A daily prayer

We ate no flesh in Eden, but afterwards,
when things got hard, we forgot
the peaceful kinship of that ancient kingdom.
As our teeth sank into their flesh
we had to deny them.
So we said
they had no souls, no reason, no thumbs,
no speech. We were so different. We made
a chain of things to protect us—fire, medicine,
our locking houses, many kinds of clothes.
And we renamed them—farm product, fur crop,
renewable resource. Pray that we will see
their faces again in the mirror of creation,
the miracle of animals, their clear eyes
meaning more than profit to our own!

—JEAN PEARSON
On Speaking Terms with Earth

SOUTHERN ELEPHANT SEAL. KING GEORGE ISLAND, ANTARCTICA. SHARON CHESTER.

T HE MAIN FACT about wolves had grown upon us slowly. Wolves have what it takes to live together in peace.

For one thing, they communicate lavishly. By gestures—the smile, for instance—and by sounds, from the big social howls to the conversational whimpers. They even seek to control by sounds first, not by biting. A full-grown wolf will plead with you not to take his possessions. And you in turn can plead with a wolf. He glances at your eyes, desists from what has displeased you and walks off as if indifferent.

—LOIS CRISLER
Arctic Wild

WOLF SONG. NOVA SCOTIA, CANADA. HEATHER PARR FENTRESS.

CECROPIA MOTH. CLERMONT COUNTY, OHIO. PRISCILLA CONNELL.

WE LOVE TO NAME and list and classify; . . . Examining each kinetic bit and calling it by name is purest gratification. Explaining the world to ourselves may be what we do best: taxonomers of the universe. We think we've grasped its moving handle when we've called its name; we think we've caught its soul. And yet a name is not sufficient to say we *know;* a classification is a bloodless device we hold up like a shield between ourselves and ignorance.

—CATHY JOHNSON
On Becoming Lost: A Naturalist's Search for Meaning

THERE IS NO QUESTION that *mind* changes the universe. Mind is as strong an evolutionary force as teeth or claws or glaciers: as influential as speech. . . . Human mind has changed the basic nature of soil, the chemical composition of air and human tissue. The ability of our minds to imagine, coupled with the ability of our hands to devise our images, brings us a power almost beyond our control—we don't know what to do with it any more, except to keep using it.

Then what is this other mind that is in the waters? These enormous alien brains that flow in the oceans—giving rise to songs, dreaming, catching at the thin web of memory, instructing each other in manners and morals—what is in the mind world of a creature with a brain bigger and possibly more complex than ours, who cannot act out its will to change the world, if only for the simple reason that it hasn't any hands?

—JOAN MCINTYRE
Mind in the Waters: A Book to Celebrate the Consciousness of Whales and Dolphins

DOLPHIN MOTHER AND CALF. MONKEY MIA, WESTERN AUSTRALIA. DEBRA GLASGOW.

CHAPMAN'S ZEBRAS. ETOSHA NATIONAL PARK, NAMIBIA. PHYLLIS GREENBERG.

EVOLUTION LOVES DEATH more than it loves you or me. This is easy to write, easy to read, and hard to believe. The words are simple, the concept clear—but you don't believe it, do you? Nor do I. How could I, when we're both so lovable? Are my values then so diametrically opposed to those that nature preserves? This is the key point.

—ANNIE DILLARD
Pilgrim at Tinker Creek

WILDEBEEST BIRTHING. NGORONGORO CRATER, TANZANIA. KATHY WATKINS.

Animals were the teachers of the first humans—showing them what to eat for food; plants to eat for medicine and how to live and even how to die. Animals continue to teach us if we give them a chance. We can learn far more from watching an animal in the wild (when it is involved with its mammalian relationships with all around it) than from cutting it up into pieces in a laboratory to study how a chemical works inside it . . . and thereby killing it.

—DOLORES LACHAPELLE
Sacred Land, Sacred Sex: Rapture of the Deep

PERHAPS THE MAJOR difference between the way non-technological peoples see animal nature and the way we see it, is that we have abstracted out of it all contradictory qualities. We look at creatures as single purpose units; they do *this* for *that* reason. The American Indian, the Congo pygmy, the Siberian shaman, recognize the contradictory livingness in animal life; understand that an animal can be both/and/or. That is, an animal can be something to eat/something that embodies wisdom other than human/something that participates in the spiritual life of the community/friend/enemy/trickster/ghost. A non-technological hunter/gatherer would never get stuck in the "logical" dilemma that "you can't love animals if you eat meat." It is this openness to the coexistence of all qualities that characterizes the "primitive" view of the living world.

—JOAN MCINTYRE

Mind in the Waters: A Book to Celebrate the Consciousness of Whales and Dolphins

POLAR BEAR JUMPING IN ICE FLOE. WAGER BAY, NORTHWEST TERRITORIES, CANADA. KATHY WATKINS.

BOBCAT. NORTHERN MONTANA, NEAR CANADIAN BORDER. PEGGY BAUER.

. . . the screaming catlike sound that wakes us every few nights is a bobcat crouched in the apple tree.

Bobcats are small, weighing only twenty pounds or so, with short tails and long, rabbity back feet. They can nurse two small litters of kittens a year. "She's meaner than a cotton sack full of wildcats," I heard a cowboy say about a woman he'd met in the bar the night before. A famous riverman's boast from the paddlewheel days on the Mississippi goes this way: "I'm all man, save what's wildcat and extra lightning." *Les chats sauvages,* the French call them, but their savagery impresses me much less than their acrobatic skills. Bobcats will kill a doe by falling on her from a tree and riding her shoulders as she runs, reaching around and scratching her face until she falls. But just as I was falling asleep again, I thought I heard the bobcat purring.

—GRETEL EHRLICH
The Solace of Open Spaces

Prayer for Reptiles

God, keep all claw-denned alligators
Free.
Keep snake and lizard, tortoise, toad,
All creep-crawl
Tip-toe turtles
Where they stand,
Keep these;
All smile-mouthed crocodiles,
Young taut-skinned, sun-wet
Creatures of the sea,
Thin, indecisive hoppers
Of the shore,
Keep these;
All hurt, haunt, hungry
Reptiles
Wandering the marge,
All land-confused
Amphibians,
Sea-driven,
Keep these;
Keep snakes, toads, lizards
All hop, all crawl, all climb,
Keep these,
Keep these.

—PATRICIA HUBBELL
8 A.M. Shadows

PYTHON. BOULDER, COLORADO. JENNY HAGER.

NESTING WANDERING ALBATROSS. ALBATROSS ISLAND, ANTARCTICA. SHARON CHESTER.

ALBATROSSES DO NEST, preferring out-of-the-way places, but they spend most of their lives on the wing, wandering the world's oceans. . . . But when albatrosses do return to land they use its green stage for all it's worth. Their courtship involves long, elaborate Oriental-looking dances, full of kissing and caressing and posing like Kabuki dancers, and symphonic mating calls, which echo from the hillsides where they nest. Observers become enchanted with their beauty and their behavior. Their names reflect the majesty and romance that people have found in them, translating into marvels like "pale-backed moon goddess."

—DIANE ACKERMAN
The New Yorker Magazine

WHAT WE MAY MISS in human interaction here we make up for by rubbing elbows with wild animals. Their florid, temperamental lives parallel ours, as do their imperfect societies. They fight and bicker, show off, and make love. I watched a Big Horn ram in rut chase a ewe around a tree for an hour. When he caught and mounted her, his horns hit a low branch and he fell off. She ran away with a younger ram in pursuit. The last I saw of them, she was headed for a dense thicket of willows and the old ram was peering through the maze looking for her.

—GRETEL EHRLICH
The Solace of Open Spaces

BIGHORN RAMS. GALLATIN RANGE, GALLATIN NATIONAL FOREST, MONTANA. DEBI OTTINGER.

WOMAN AND TREE FERN. OHIO FOREST, VOLCANO NATIONAL PARK, HAWAII. PAM ROBERSON.

HUMAN REALM

We know ourselves to be made from this earth.
We know this earth is made from our bodies.
For we see ourselves. And we are nature. We are
nature seeing nature. We are nature with a
concept of nature. Nature weeping. Nature
speaking of nature to nature.

—SUSAN GRIFFIN
Woman and Nature: The Roaring Inside Her

FISHERMAN AT DUSK. BALI. PAM ROBERSON.

Work is the country of hands, and they want to live there in the dailiness of it, the repetition that is time's language of prayer, a common tongue.

—LINDA HOGAN
"Waking Up the Rake"

Our Life as Gaia

from Thinking Like a Mountain: Towards a Council of All Beings

JOANNA MACY

COME BACK WITH ME into a story we all share, a story whose rhythm beats in us still. The story belongs to each of us and to all of us, like the beat of this drum, like the heartbeat of our living universe.

There is science now to construct the story of the journey we have made on this earth, the story that connects us with all beings. There is also great yearning and great need to own that story—to break out of our isolation as persons and as a species and recover through that story our larger identity. The challenge to do that now and burst out of the separate prison cells of our contrivings, is perhaps the most wonderful aspect of our being alive today.

Right now on our planet we need to remember that story—to harvest it and taste it. For we are in a hard time, a fearful time. And it is the knowledge of the bigger story that is going to carry us through. It can give us the courage, it can give us the strength, it can give us the hilarity to dance our people into a world of sanity. Let us remember it together.

With the heartbeat of the drum we hear the rhythm that underlies all our days and doings. Throughout our sleeping and rising, through all our working and loving, our heart has been beating steady, steady. That steady sturdy inner sound has accompanied us all the way. And so it can take us back now, back through our lives, back through our childhood, back through our birth. In our mother's womb there was that same sound, that same beat, as we floated there in the fluid right under her heart.

Let that beat take us back farther still. Let's go back, back far beyond our conception in this body, back to the first splitting and spinning of the stars. As scientists measure now, it is fifteen billion years ago we manifested—in what they call the Big Bang.

There we were, careening out through space and time, creating space and time. Slowly, with the speed of light, in vast curls of flame and darkness, we reached for form. We were then great swirls of clouds and gas and dancing particles—can you imagine you remember? And the particles, as they circled in the dance, desired each other and formed atoms. It is the same desire for form that beats now in this drum and in our hearts.

Ten billion years later, one of the most beautiful swirls of that swirling mass split off from its blazing sun—the sun we feel now on our faces—and became the form we know best. And our lifetime as Gaia began.

Touch our Earth, touch Gaia.

Touch Gaia again by touching your face, that is Gaia, too.

Touch Gaia again by touching your sister and brother. That is Gaia too.

In the immediate planet-time of ours, Gaia is becoming aware of herself, she is finding out who she is. How rich she is in the multitudinous and exquisite forms she takes.

Let us imagine that her life—*our* life as our planet—could be condensed into twenty-four hours, beginning at midnight. Until five o'clock the following afternoon all her adventures are geological. All was volcanic flamings and steaming rains washing over the shifting bones of the continents into shifting seas—only at five o'clock comes organic life.

To the heartbeat of life in you and this drum, you too, right now, can shift a bit—shift free from identifying solely with your latest human form. The fire of those early volcanoes, the strength of those tectonic plates, is in us still. And it may well be, if things continue the way they are going, that we will all return for a spell to non-organic life. We'd be radioactive for quite a while, but we are built to endure.

For now and in these very bodies of ours, we carry traces of Gaia's story as organic life. We were aquatic first, as we remember in our mother's womb, growing vestigial gills and fins. The salt from those early seas flows still in our sweat and tears. And the age of the dinosaurs we carry with us, too, in our reptilian brain, situated so conveniently at the end of our spinal column. Complex organic life was learning to protect itself and it is all right there in our neurological system, in the rush of instinct to flee or fight.

And when did we appear as mammals? In those twenty-four hours of Gaia's life, it was at 11:30 PM! And when did we become human? One second to midnight.

Now let us take that second to midnight that is our story as humans and reckon that, in turn, as twenty-four hours. Let's look back through the twenty-four hours that we have been human.

Beginning at midnight and until two o'clock in the afternoon, we live in small groups in Africa. Can you imagine you remember? We feel pretty vulnerable; we haven't the speed of the other creatures, or their claws or fangs or natural armor. But we have our remarkable hands, opposable thumbs to help shape tools and weapons. And we have in our throats and frontal lobes the capacity for speech. Grunts and shouts turn into language as we collaborate in strategies and rituals. Those days and nights on the verge of the forests, as we weave baskets and stories around our fires, represent the biggest hunk of our human experience.

Then in small bands we begin branching out. We move across the face of Gaia; we learn to face the cold and hunt the mammoth and name the trees of the northern forests, the flowers and seasons of the tundra. We know it is Gaia by whom we live and we carve her in awe and fear and gratitude, giving her our breasts and hips. When we settle into agriculture, when we begin domesticating animals and fencing off our croplands and deciding that they could be owned as private property, when we build great cities with granaries and temples and observatories to chart the stars, the time is eleven fifty-eight. Two minutes to midnight.

At eleven fifty-nine comes a time of quickening change: we want to chart the stars within as well as those we see in the skies; we want to seek the authority of inner experience. To free the questing mind we set it apart from Gaia. We make conjectures and rules and heroes to help us chart our freedoms to think and act. The great religions of our planet-time arise. At six seconds to midnight comes a man called Buddha and shortly after another called Jesus of Nazareth.

What now shapes our world—our industrial society with its bombs and bulldozers—has taken place in the last few microseconds of the day we have known as humans.

Yet those few microseconds bring us right to the brink of time. And each of us knows that. Each of us, at some level of our awareness, knows that we are doing ourselves in—that Gaia herself, our self, is in danger. And at some level of your consciousness that is why you are here. Oh yes, you may think you are here to heal yourselves on the personal level and find your power in terms of your individual lives. True enough. But we are also here because we know our planet is in danger and all life on it could go—like that! And we fear that this knowledge might drive us insane if we let it in.

Much of the time it is hard to believe that we have come to this—to such an apocalyptic moment. Even those of us who work hard to stop nuclear weapons have trouble really believing that they exist. After the millions of years of life on earth, after the millennia of our civilizations, after Ishtar and Shakespeare and

Gandhi and Dorothy Day, we find it hard to credit the fact that we are deliberately manufacturing and deploying these weapons, targeting them at great populations, posing them on hair-trigger alert, leaving them liable to go off on a computer malfunction. . . .

So we are now at a point unlike any other in our story. I suspect we have, in some way, chosen to be here at this culminating chapter or turning point. We have opted to be alive when the stakes are high, to test everything we have ever learned about interconnectedness, about courage—to test it now when Gaia is ailing and her children are ill. We are alive right now when it could be curtains for conscious life on this beautiful water planet hanging there like a jewel in space. Our foremothers and forefathers faced nothing quite like this, because every generation before us took it for granted that life would continue. Each lived with that tacit assumption. Personal death, wars, plagues were ever encompassed in that larger assurance that life would continue. That assurance is lost now and we are alive at the time of that great loss. It is not the loss of the future. It is the loss of the certainty that there will be a future. It affects everyone, whether they work in the Pentagon or the peace movement. And the toll it takes has barely begun to be measured.

In so-called primitive societies rites of passage are held for adolescents, because it is in adolescence that the fact of personal death or mortality is integrated into the personality. The individual goes through the prescribed ordeal of the initiation rite in order to integrate that knowledge, so that he or she can assume the rights and responsibilities of adulthood. That is what we are doing right now on the collective level, in this planet-time. We are confronting and integrating into our awareness our collective mortality as a species. We must do that so that we can wake up and assume the rights and responsibilities of planetary adulthood—so that we can grow up! That is, in a sense, what we are doing here.

When you go out from here, please keep listening to the drumbeat. You will hear it in your heart. And as you hear it, remember that it is the heartbeat of the universe as well, and of Gaia your planet and your larger Self.

When you return to your communities to organize, saying no to the machinery of death and yes to life, remember your true identity. Remember your story, our story. Clothe yourself in your true authority. You speak not only as yourself or for yourself. You were not born yesterday. You have been through many dyings and know in your heartbeat and bones the precarious, exquisite balance of life. Out of that knowledge you can speak and act. You will speak and act with the courage and endurance that has been yours through the long, beautiful aeons of your life story as Gaia.

DANCER IN TRADITIONAL DRESS. CROWN MINE, NEAR JOHANNESBURG, SO. AFRICA. RITA SUMMERS.

Where there is woman there is magic.
—NTOZAKE SHANGE
Sassafras, Cypress & Indigo

The truest expression of a people is in its dances and its music. Bodies never lie.

—AGNES DEMILLE
"Do I Hear a Waltz?"

MEN'S TRADITIONAL DANCER, STANDOFF POWWOW. ALBERTA, CANADA. KATHLEEN NORRIS COOK.

FOLK-CRAFT ARTIST AT HIDA FOLKLORE MUSEUM AND OLD HOUSE RESERVATION. TAKAYAMA, JAPAN. LARA HARTLEY.

A s a human being I am a great meddler; I fiddle, alter, modify. This is neither good nor bad, merely human, in the same way that the snake who eats mice and phoebes is merely serpentish. But being human I have the kind of mind which can recognize that when I fiddle and twitch any part of the circle there are reverberations throughout the whole.

—SUE HUBBELL
A Country Year: Living the Questions

KUNA WOMAN WITH PIPE AND PARAKEET. ACUATUPU ISLAND, PANAMA. SHARON CHESTER.

"I AM NOT LIKE YOU," the old woman said slowly. "I do not tell stories. I see visions. I see that life is not a line but a circle. Why do men imagine for themselves the illusory freedom of a soaring mind, so that the body of nature becomes a cage? 'Tis not true. To be human is to be circled in the cycles of nature, rooted in the processes that nurture us in life, breathing in and breathing out human life just as plants breathe in and out their photosynthesis. . . ."

—ELIZABETH DODSON GRAY
Green Paradise Lost

EVERY THREE DAYS or so white pastures glide overhead and drop themselves like skeins of hair to earth. The Chinese call snow that has drifted "white jade mountains," but winter looks oceanic to me. Snow swells, drops back, and hits the hulls of our lives with a course-bending sound.

—GRETEL EHRLICH
The Solace of Open Spaces

EARLY MORNING IN THE KHUMBU ICEFALL. MOUNT EVEREST, NEPAL. ARLENE BLUM.

THREE LITTLE GIRLS. LITTLETON, COLORADO. SUSAN WORTH JENKINS.

A CHILD'S WORLD IS fresh and new and beautiful, full of wonder and excitement. It is our misfortune that for most of us that clear-eyed vision, that true instinct for what is beautiful and awe-inspiring, is dimmed and even lost before we reach adulthood. If I had influence with the good fairy who is supposed to preside over the christening of all children I should ask that her gift to each child in the world be a sense of wonder so indestructible that it would last throughout life, as an unfailing antidote against the boredom and disenchantments of later years, the sterile preoccupation with things that are artificial, the alienation from the sources of our strength.

—RACHEL CARSON
A Sense of Wonder

IN CHINA . . . Taoist temples were called *kuan,* meaning "to see," such was the importance to them of seeing nature. The first Japanese to go to China to study Buddhism and bring it back to their native land, were thus deeply influenced by this necessity of turning to nature in order to see. For instance, when Dogen left China to return to Japan, his master told him to avoid cities and keep away from government: "Just live in deep mountains and dark valleys." Dogen returned to Japan and headed for the mountains of Echizen Province where he founded the Soto Zen school of Buddhism in 1224.

—DOLORES LACHAPPELE
Sacred Land, Sacred Sex: Rapture of the Deep

SHINTO PRIEST AT DAWN. HONSHU, JAPAN. PAM ROBERSON.

DAWN ON LI RIVER. NEAR GUILIN, CHINA. HEATHER ANGEL.

ONENESS

. . . to understand another human being you must gain some insight into the conditions which made him what he is.

—MARGARET BOURKE-WHITE
quoted in *The Woman's Eye,*
by Anne Tucker

PINK PHLOX AND CHAIR IN GARDEN. ZACHARY, LOUISIANA. NANCY WEBB.

after the garden party   the garden
—RUTH YARROW
A Journal for Reflections

The Universe Responds:
Or, How I Learned We Can Have Peace On Earth

from Living by the Word

ALICE WALKER

To SOME PEOPLE who read the following there will seem to be something special or perhaps strange about me. I have sometimes felt this way myself. To others, however, what I am about to write will appear obvious. I think our response to "strangeness" or "specialness" depends on where we are born, where we are raised, how much idle time we have had to watch trees (long enough at least to notice there is not an ugly one among them) swaying in the wind. Or to watch rivers, rainstorms, or the sea.

A few years ago I wrote an essay called "Everything Is a Human Being," which explores to some extent the Native American view that all of creation is of one substance and therefore deserving of the same respect. I described the death of a snake that I caused and wrote of my remorse. I wrote the piece to celebrate the birth of Martin Luther King, Jr., and I read it first to a large group of college students in California. I also read it other places, so that by summer (I had written it in winter) it had been read three or four times, and because I cannot bear to repeat myself very much, I put it away.

That summer "my" land in the country crawled with snakes. There was always the large resident snake, whom my mother named "Susie," crawling about in the area that marks the entrance to my studio. But there were also lots of others wherever we looked. A black-and-white king snake appeared underneath the shower stall in the garden. A striped red-and-black one, very pretty, appeared near the pond. It now revealed the little hole in the ground in which it lived by lying half in and half out of it as it basked in the sun. Garden snakes crawled up and down the roads and paths. One day, leaving my house with a box of books in his arms, my companion literally tripped over one of these.

We spoke to all these snakes in friendly voices. They went their way. We went ours. After about a two-week bloom of snakes, we seemed to have our usual number; just Susie and a couple of her children.

A few years later, I wrote an essay about a horse called Blue. It was about how humans treat horses and other animals; how hard it is for us to see them as the suffering, fully conscious, enslaved beings they are. It also marked the beginning of my effort to become non-meat-eating (fairly successful). After reading this essay in public only once, this is what happened. A white horse came and settled herself on the land. (Her owner, a neighbor, soon came to move her.) The two horses on the ranch across the road began to run up to their fence whenever I passed, leaning over it and making what sounded to my ears like joyful noises. They had never done this before (I checked with the human beings I lived with to be sure of this), and after a few more times of greeting me as if I'd done something especially nice for them, they stopped. Now when I pass they look at me with the same reserve they did before. But there is still a spark of *recognition*.

What to make of this?

What I have noticed in my small world is that if I praise the wild flowers growing on the hill in front of my house, the following year they double in profusion and brilliance. If I admire the squirrel that swings from branch to branch outside my window, pretty soon I have three or four squirrels to admire. If I look into the eyes of a raccoon that has awakened me by noisily rummaging through the garbage at night, and acknowledge that it looks maddeningly like a mischievous person—paws on hips, masked eyes, a certain impudent stance, as it looks back at me—I soon have a family of raccoons living in a tree a few yards off my deck. (From this tree they easily forage in the orchard at night and eat, or at least take bites out of, all the apples. Which is not fun. But that is another story.)

And then, too, there are the deer, who know they need never, ever fear me.

In white-directed movies about the Indians of the Old West, you sometimes see the "Indians" doing a rain dance, a means of praying for rain. The message delivered by the moviemaker is that such dancing and praying is ridiculous, that either it will rain or it will not. All white men know this. The Indians are backward and stupid and wasting their time. But there is also that last page or so in the story of Black Elk, in which his anthropologist/friend John Neihart goes with him on a last visit to the Badlands to pray atop Harney Peak, a place sacred to the Sioux. It is a cloudless day, but the ancient Black Elk hopes that the Great Spirit, as in the real "old" days, will acknowledge his prayer for the good of his people by sending at least a few drops of rain. As he prays, in his old, tired voice, mostly of his love of the Universe and his failure to be perfect, a small cloud indeed forms. It rains, just enough to say "Yes." Then the sky clears. Even today there is the belief among many indigenous holy people that when a person of goodness dies, the Universe acknowledges the spirit's departure by sending storms and rain.

The truth is in the country, where I live much of the time, I am virtually overrun by birds and animals—raccoons, snakes, deer, horses (occasionally). During a recent court trial at which a neighbor and I both happened to find ourselves, her opening words of greeting included the information that two wild pigs she'd somehow captured had broken out and were, she feared, holed up somewhere on my land.

But at least, I thought, my house in the city is safe.

But no.

One night after dinner, as some friends were leaving my house, I opened my front door, only to have a large black dog walk gratefully inside. It had obviously been waiting quietly on the stoop. It came into the hallway, sniffed my hands, and prepared to make itself at home, exactly as if it had lived in my house all its life. There was no nervousness whatsoever about being an intruder. No, no, I said, out you go! It did not want to go, but my friends and I persuaded it. It settled itself at the door and there it stayed, barking reproachfully until I went to bed. Very late that night I heard its owners calling it. George! they called. George! Here, George! They were cursing and laughing. Drunk. George made no response.

I suddenly realized that George was not lost. He had run away. He had run away from these cursing, laughing drunks who were now trying to find him. This realization meant the end of sleep for me that night as I lay awake considering my responsibility to George. (I felt none toward his owners.) For George obviously "knew" which house was at least *supposed* to be a stop on the underground railroad, and had come to it; but I, in my city house, had refused to acknowledge my house as such. If I let it in, where would I put it? Then, too, I'm not particularly fond of the restlessness of dogs. The way they groan and fart in their sleep, chase rabbits in their dreams, and flop themselves over, rattling their chains (i.e., collars and dog tags). George had run away from these drunks who "owned" him, people no doubt unfit to own anything at all that breathed. Did they beat him? Did they tie him to trees and lampposts outside pubs (as I've so often seen done) while they went inside and had drink after drink? Were all the "lost" dogs one heard about really runaways? It hit me with great force that a dog I had once had, Myshkin, had undoubtedly run away from the small enclosed backyard in which he had been kept and in which he was probably going mad, whereas I had for years indulged in the fantasy that he'd been stolen! No dog in his right mind would voluntarily leave a cushy prison run by loving humans, right?

Or suppose George was a woman, beaten or psychologically abused by her spouse. What then? Would I let her in? I would, wouldn't I? But where to put George, anyway? If I put him in the cellar, he might bark. I hate the sound of barking. If I put him in the parlor, he might spread fleas. Who was this dog, anyway?

George stayed at my door the whole night. In the morning I heard him bark, but by the time I was up, he was gone.

I think I am telling you that the animals of the planet are in desperate peril, and they are fully aware of this. No less than human beings are doing in all parts of the world, they are seeking sanctuary. But I am also telling you that we are connected to them at least as intimately as we are connected to trees. Without plant life human beings could not breathe. Plants produce oxygen. Without free animal life I believe we will lose the spiritual equivalent of oxygen. "Magic," intuition, sheer astonishment at the forms the Universe devises in which to express life—itself—will no longer be able to breathe in us. One day it occurred to me that if all the birds died, as they might well do, eventually, from the poisoning of their air, water, and food, it would be next to impossible to describe to our children the wonder of their flight. To most children, I think, the flight of a bird—if they've never seen one fly—would be imagined as stiff and unplayful, like the flight of an airplane.

But what I'm also sharing with you is this thought: The Universe responds. What you ask of it, it gives. The military-industrial complex and its leaders and scientists have shown more faith in this reality than have those of us who do not believe in war and who want peace. They have asked the Earth for all its deadlier substances. They have been confident in their faith in hatred and war. The Universe, ever responsive, the Earth, ever giving, has opened itself fully to their desires. Ironically, Black Elk and nuclear scientists can be viewed in much the same way: as men who received from it a sign reflective of their own hearts.

I remember when I used to dismiss the bumper sticker "Pray for Peace." I realize now that I did not understand it, since I also did not understand prayer; which I now know to be the active affirmation in the physical world of our inseparableness from the divine; and everything, *especially* the physical world, is divine. War will stop when we no longer praise it, or give it any attention at all. Peace will come wherever it is sincerely invited. Love will overflow every sanctuary given it. Truth will grow where the fertilizer that nourishes it is also truth. Faith will be its own reward.

Believing this, which I learned from my experience with the animals and the wild flowers, I have found that my fear of nuclear destruction has been to a degree lessened. I know perfectly well that we may all die, and relatively soon, in a global holocaust, which was first imprinted, probably against their wishes, on the hearts of the scientist fathers of the atomic bomb, no doubt deeply wounded and frightened human beings; but I also know we have the power, as all the Earth's people, to conjure up the healing rain imprinted on Black Elk's heart. Our death is in our hands.

Knock and the door shall be opened. Ask and you shall receive.

Whatsoever you do to the least of these, you do also unto me—and to yourself. For we are one.

"God" answers prayers. Which is another way of saying, "the Universe responds."

We are *indeed* the world. Only if we have reason to fear what is in our hearts need we fear for the planet. Teach yourself peace.

Pass it on.

What the Ancient Ones Knew

Petroglyphs in the rock:
a woman balancing a world

in each outstretched hand.
The worlds spin in place.

She stares across
the valley at winter peaks

floating in clouds. A small
smile lightens her face.

Her feet ground the earth.
Her head grazes the sky.

To her right side coyote tosses
the moon off the end of his nose

and barks at the close of night.
As the hot sun dries her face

the woman moves her left hand
forward and offers me a world.

"Here," she says, "let it spin.
It will weave its own fabric."

—GAYLE LAURADUNN

FIVE FACES PICTOGRAPH. CANYONLANDS NATIONAL PARK, UTAH. LINDE WAIDHOFER.

Sandstone Sculpture. Jurassic Sandstone, Colorado Plateau. Linde Waidhofer.

WE ARE THE LAND. To the best of my understanding, that is the fundamental idea that permeates American Indian life; the land (Mother) and the people (mothers) are the same. . . . The land is not really a place, separate from ourselves, where we act out the drama of our isolate destinies; . . . The earth is not a mere source of survival, distant from the creatures it nurtures and from the spirit that breathes in us, nor is it to be considered an inert resource on which we draw in order to keep our ideological self functioning, whether we perceive that self in sociological or personal terms. . . . Rather, for American Indians . . . the earth *is* being, as all creatures are also being: aware, palpable, intelligent, alive.

—PAULA GUNN ALLEN
The Sacred Hoop

VERMONT POND IN AUTUMN. SONJA BULLATY.

autumn stream:
a yellow reflection rises
to meet its leaf
—RUTH YARROW
A Journal for Reflections

BIGHORN SHEEP ON SYNCLINE RIDGE. JASPER NATIONAL PARK, ALBERTA, CANADA. ESTHER SCHMIDT.

THE RAM TAKES almost ten minutes to come down the hillside. After reading about their prowess in leaping rocks and sheer cliffs, covering ground with astonishing leaps and bounds, I am struck by his extreme deliberateness, which I take also to be a measure of his serenity.

—ANN ZWINGER
The Mysterious Lands

TOAD AND WORM. BOONE COUNTY, MISSOURI. GAY BUMGARNER.

NATURE IS MOUTHS, or maybe a single mouth. Why glamorize it, romanticize it, well yes but we must, we're writers, poets, mystics (of a sort) aren't we, precisely what else are we to do but glamorize and romanticize and generally exaggerate the significance of anything we focus the white heat of our "creativity" upon . . . ? And why not Nature, since it's there, common property, mute, can't talk back, allows us the possibility of transcending the human condition for a while, writing prettily of mountain ranges, white-tailed deer, the purple crocuses outside this very window, the thrumming dazzling "life-force" we imagine we all support. Why not.

Nature *is* more than a mouth—it's a dazzling variety of mouths. And it pleases the senses, in any case, as the physicists' chill universe of numbers certainly does not.

—JOYCE CAROL OATES
"Against Nature"

T HERE ARE SEVEN or eight categories of phenomena in the world that are worth
talking about, and one of them is weather. Any time you care to get in your car
and drive across the country and over the mountains, come into our valley, . . . drive
up the road to the house, walk across the yard, knock on the door and ask to come in
and talk about the weather, you'd be welcome.

—ANNIE DILLARD
Pilgrim at Tinker Creek

CLOUD BANK OVER MOUNTAIN. ISLE OF SKYE, SCOTLAND. SONJA BULLATY.

KITE AND PELICANS. MARIN COUNTY COAST, CALIFORNIA. GAY BUMGARNER.

In coming close to earth I have come close to heaven.
—GILEAN DAVIS
Silence Is My Homeland

SUNSET AND CYPRESS. BIG CYPRESS NATIONAL PRESERVE/EVERGLADES NATIONAL PARK, FLORIDA. BARBARA BRUNDEGE.

Trees stir memories; live waters heal them.
—ANNIE DILLARD
Pilgrim at Tinker Creek

Hindu Chant (Stanza 4)

My Mother is everywhere . . .
In the perfume of a rose,
The eyes of a tiger,
The pages of a book,
The food we partake,
The whistling wind of the desert,
The blazing gems of the sunset,
The crystal light of the full moon,
The opal veils of sunrise.

—GRACE GALLATIN SETON
The Singing Traveler

SHAKTI CARVING, SHORE TEMPLE. MAMMALLAPURAM, TAMIL NADU, INDIA. JUDITH BOICE.

Be a gardener.
Dig a ditch,
toil and sweat,
and turn the earth upside down
and seek the deepness
and water the plants in time.
Continue this labor
and make sweet floods to run
and noble and abundant fruits
to spring.
Take this food and drink
and carry it to God
as your true worship.

—JULIAN OF NORWICH
Meditations with Julian of Norwich

LAVENDER FIELD. PROVENCE, FRANCE. SONJA BULLATY.

HAYSTACKS IN THE BAVARIAN ALPS. BARBARA A. MILLER

I HAVE FELT LOVE like a force—a strange love of landscape itself, of the earth
beneath my feet—welling up and overflowing and exploding along the capillaries
of my brain until I wanted to run free, not stopping until I could run no more, until
I dropped like a stone and lay in place until the next glacier moved me.

—CATHY JOHNSON
On Becoming Lost: A Naturalist's Search for Meaning

THE PASSION TO SEE:
ABOUT THE PHOTOGRAPHERS

HEATHER ANGEL
Born July 21, 1941, in Buckinghamshire, England.
"Nothing can compare with the excitement of being in a wilderness situation capturing aspects of animal behavior. Working as a wildlife photographer has taken me to many remote parts of the world which I know I would never have seen if I had remained a marine biologist. Today, wildlife and nature photographs play an essential part in communicating to a wide audience those species and habitats that are under threat by the hand of man. The aim of my pictures is to stimulate a greater awareness of the splendor and diversity, as well as the fragility, of life on Earth."

PEGGY BAUER
Born March 2, 1932, in Riverside, Illinois.
"Photography only began when I married Erwin Bauer, who was already known in the field. He patiently taught me what I needed to know and together we went to places that would inspire a rock. . . . now (twenty years later) we are full partners in our nature photography business. So although I'm nearing sixty and Erwin has been on Social Security for several years now, we are as enthusiastic about photography as we ever were and have no plans to stop. Ever."

ARLENE BLUM
Born March 1, 1945, in Davenport, Iowa.
"The stark beauty of the highest mountains has motivated both my climbing and my photography. Maybe if my images were satisfying enough, I could just enjoy the mountains through my photos and quit having to risk my life going up there again and again. Currently, my photography is mostly centered on my four-year-old daughter. For me, she is just as beautiful and challenging as the high Himalaya—and lots more fun!"

JUDITH BOICE

Born March 20, 1962, in Toledo, Ohio.

"Photography is an offshoot of my love for wilderness, not my primary motivation for traveling and living in remote areas. I experience beauty and life in a much more direct, profound way in wilderness areas. I hope that my photographs may touch and change people, just as the Earth has shaped and transformed me."

BARBARA BRUNDEGE

Born August 29, 1950, in Walton, New York.

"As a young girl, I spent many hours with my family in the woods of upstate New York observing wildlife and learning about the flora and fauna. From these outings, my curiosity grew about animal behavior and the natural history of plants and trees. Photographing the Earth and its inhabitants continually feeds my curiosity, my intellect, and my spirit. In return for the great gifts the land has given me, I hope my photographs inspire others to care for and preserve our beautiful land for future generations."

SONJA BULLATY

Born in Prague, Czechoslovakia.

Born in Czechoslovakia 14 years before the Nazi invasion of Prague, Sonja was the only member of her [Jewish] family to survive the Holocaust of World War II. For Sonja, landscape photography became "a very important way to express what I feel about the world. When you have seen the depths of horror, you are so much more responsive to enormous joy. I have often felt that the reason I celebrate life and beauty is precisely because I have seen so much pain and ugliness."

GAY BUMGARNER

Born in Independence, Missouri.

Gay, a professional landscape designer, found that her interest "in animals and birds became more pressing than landscapes. I am entranced by the surprises and mystifying behavior I see from my blinds when animals coexist and cooperate. You could never have a field with one animal in it; they are always interacting with each other. The worm is the same size as the toad—they have the same significance."

KATHLEEN THORMOD CARR

Born May 24, 1946, in Los Angeles, California.

"I am fascinated by the energy I sense within the forms I am photographing. Using a variety of techniques, I attempt to express this presence more tangibly. When I take time to really see, I am filled with wonder at the mystery and perfection in nature and in people. I want my photography to inspire people to take better care of our Mother Earth and each other."

SHARON CHESTER
Born in Chicago, Illinois.

The first woman to see all the bird families in the world, Sharon comments that her photographs "do not epitomize hard work or great skill—images just seem to climb into my camera. . . . Remote location photography can present a few hazards, like being stranded overnight on an uninhabited island when my Zodiac [boat] overturned in an antarctic storm. I've been chased in and through a Volkswagen by a lovesick boar, pushed away from a campsite by a hungry bear, and 'rained on' by a territorial male howler monkey. A biologist's eye and an ability to appreciate the humor of such situations may be the secret to my achievements."

PRISCILLA CONNELL
Born in Cincinnati, Ohio.

"I am rather passionate about photography and all that it entails—from the basics of getting in the field with the right equipment for the job at hand to everything I need to create the 'perfect' image—that is, learned techniques, both mechanical and compositional, together with an eye for not only 'looking' but 'seeing.' I hope that I expose the film at the right time and in the right light before the picture vanishes forever."

KATHLEEN NORRIS COOK
Born November 23, 1941, in Jennings, Louisiana.

"Photography is discipline and patience, but more importantly for me, it is also the means by which I am able to be a part of the magic of nature. I think of these times as gifts from the Universe. They are the most compelling and usually the most outrageous in terms of beauty and feeling. It is nature in its wildest splendor giving proof of the creative power that is in all things."

MARTHA L. DAVIS
Born August 20, 1953, in Dallas, Oregon.

"As a photographer, I find that my biologist's eye is drawn to details, both for their own beauty and as representatives of a larger whole, whose interconnections are not always easily perceived. The thing that excites me about this work is the chance to communicate, to share my love of the beauty and intricacies of the natural world, to show others how and what I see in a place, time, or thing, and to share my vision of the world and how it works."

HEATHER PARR FENTRESS
Born November 11, 1948, in Portland, Oregon.

"Still photography is like poetry, rather than a novel—it gives you the *feeling* of motion. . . . I photograph because of a sense of wholeness. I never begin photographing right away; I need to hit a level of comfort and then go more and more deeply into it. The more deeply I know one thing, the more I know other things, as well. I concentrate on what I am seeing and try to capture *that* moment."

DEBRA GLASGOW
Born November 25, 1957, in Morrinsville, New Zealand.

"I photograph in an attempt to share a moment of intense realization, of wonder, of awe. Perhaps, too, I seek to teach respect. I wish to show beauty in the hope of prompting a more nurturing response to our world. I think an ounce of empathy could go a long way to solving a lot of problems we face today."

PHYLLIS GREENBERG
Born March 3, 1927, in Brooklyn, New York.

"We live in a very beautiful world filled with fascinating creatures of all sizes, shapes, and colors. There is so much to see and to learn that if I lived for another hundred years I would not run out of subjects. Every day I spend in the field photographing is a joy, so I have never minded any of the discomforts that sometimes occur in my endeavor to capture a small piece of this world on film. I hope that I can continue doing this for at least another twenty-five years."

JENNY HAGER
Born September 14, 1955, in Pittsburgh, Pennsylvania.

Following a career as an outdoor educator, climber, and guide, Jenny's lifestyle changed "with marriage and a baby. . . . This renewed my commitment to nature photography, wherever I found it. It's much more exciting to show people the beauty they see every day, if they take the time to look, than to record places that are so obviously gorgeous and cannot be overlooked."

LARA HARTLEY
Born October 13, 1946, in West Palm Beach, Florida.

"From the beginning, photography was a documenting of what was—not a creating of something from nothing, but an attempt to see reality. . . . I wanted my work to expose social injustices and to provide an avenue for change. Pretty lofty goals for an aspiring shooter. After twenty-two years I still document what is, with a bent toward making changes in the way we treat the planet . . . but I prefer my bio to read: 'Lara Hartley, Marching Band, University of Arizona, 1967.' Now that's a biography!"

SUSAN WORTH JENKINS
Born August 23, 1946, in Denver, Colorado.

"Being constantly on the lookout for subjects to photograph and new ways to look at things has greatly increased my powers of observation and enhanced the quality of my interactions with the world around me. Instead of simply documenting a subject, my approach has become a search for beauty and connectedness with whatever I photograph."

BARBARA A. MILLER
Born April 24, 1941, in Rochester, New York.

"Photography means being your own person, your own master, walking, running, climbing to your own beat. Photography is a wonderful teacher, always showing me the nuances of any scene, helping me discern when I am seeing, and when I am *not* seeing."

DEBI OTTINGER
Born October 16, 1951, in Denver, Colorado.

"Although my photography began as a hobby many years ago, my special bond with animals has been in my heart for as long as I can remember. Above my desk I have a quote by George Eliot: 'Animals are such agreeable friends . . . they ask no questions . . . they pass no criticisms.' Perhaps this is why I have always been so completely comfortable with them. It is my belief that if my audience can experience this same wildness through my eyes, they will battle to preserve it and forbid further destruction."

JOANNE PAVIA
Born November 24, 1953, in Great Bend, Kansas.

Joanne has developed a successful nature and gardening photography business. According to Joanne, "I'm not sure where I'm headed next, possibly . . . photographing animals and expressing my feelings about the spirit of nature and its power. And lately, people have been asking me if I photograph people—a hint?"

PAMELA ROBERSON
Born June 5, 1948, in Washington, D.C.

"I think photography is about arresting stillness so we focus on the subject with our full attention. Only when I look fully upon something do I feel my mind is absolutely as awake as possible, in my present state of consciousness. Focusing on an object has been a Tibetan meditation technique for centuries. In many ways, I and other photographers— as opposed to video, television, or cinema viewers—are throwbacks."

ESTHER SCHMIDT
Born August 20, 1922, in Victoria, British Columbia, Canada.
Together with her husband, Dennis, Esther has developed a successful photographic business and published two books. "But even more thrilling is to be accepted by wild animals in their own territory. Once, after spending several days photographing a red fox, he came very close, showing no fear. Suddenly, he simply laid down with his head behind some short grasses. He just watched contentedly while allowing me to photograph with a normal lens."

MARY ELLEN SCHULTZ
Born September 8, 1923, in Santa Maria, California.
"I've never actively pursued photography with a special goal in mind. To clutch the muse tightly would in effect cause the gift to cease to exist. . . . The facet of photography I love most lies in the exploration of flowers, grasses, the close-up world underfoot. . . . There is great beauty there, and in the world underfoot I find the shapes and forms so beautiful, where nature truly becomes an art form."

WENDY SHATTIL
Born April 7, 1949, in Chicago, Illinois.
"As a wildlife photographer I have an outstanding opportunity to make environmental statements that can influence countless people. I feel an obligation to use my skills and opportunities to strive for just that. Just as an anthropologist observes and documents a culture, I do the same when photographing animals. Humans benefit directly or indirectly from the natural world, and we have a responsibility to interact wisely with it."

LORNA STANTON
Born May 16, 1949, in Johannesburg, South Africa.
In addition to working full-time as a photographer, Lorna founded and now runs the Bateleur Raptor Rehabilitation and Breeding Center, which rehabilitates and reintroduces birds of prey into the wild. Since 1982 she has worked for the National Parks Board. "Photography for me is not a job, but a way of life. I am fortunate enough to have a job that involves my main interest in life, which is conservation, and allows me the freedom to explore wilderness areas."

RITA SUMMERS
Born September 25, 1938, in Las Vegas, New Mexico.
"Unlike most photographers, I love to work alone and often take off for a week or two in my camper. I'm fifty-two years old and hope to be outside photographing until I'm a hundred. Then I'll come inside and paint from my photos for a few years."

BRENDA THARP
Born November 1, 1953, in Rockaway, New Jersey.
"Photography allows me to experience that which I am photographing—nature, wildlife, exotic and unique cultures. My camera is my license to be curious, to explore, to observe. The experience enriches my life and often puts it in proper perspective. I aim to share my experiences with others, to say, 'Look! Isn't it wonderful?'"

ANNIE TIBERIO
Born September 16, 1951, in Paw Paw, Michigan.
"If my photography inspires someone, somewhere, to do something positive, however small, I have made a difference. If I can help someone else with the tools to begin his or her own quest for images, and discover the same yen to slow down, understand, and hope, then I have become part of a process of bringing people into the 'fold.' I guess, in a smaller, quieter way, it is a form of activism in the environment."

CONNIE TOOPS
Born March 12, 1951, in Covington, Ohio.
"Although nature writing is now a major part of my career, it is the field work and photography that continue to be the driving force behind the projects I choose to work on. My 'love' is torn between birds and wildflowers, which are my two favorite categories of photographic subjects."

LINDE WAIDHOFER
Born January 3, 1944, in Bryan, Texas.
"I go to special places, to be with the environment and to interpret the overwhelming emotions I feel when I'm in these places. Creating photographs that I find satisfying demands great patience. In the desert, it may require going to a certain location at several different times of the year to find when the angle of the sun is best and then watching all day for the best light. But spending this amount of time ultimately is essential for understanding the essence of a place, and it is only that kind of understanding that makes a great photograph possible."

ERICA WANGSGARD
Born February 2, 1953, in New York City.
Erica enrolled in a beginning photography class, and after learning the basic technical process, "I immediately began painting and drawing on my prints. Some results were horrific; some were very exciting. Photographers accused me of 'contaminating' my photographs. I instantly knew I was doing the right thing. I had made an amazing discovery about myself: I loved the challenge of balancing painting and the silver image."

KATHY WATKINS
Born March 11, 1960, in Craik, Saskatchewan, Canada.
"I've lived a lot of my professional career as a registered nurse in the far north of Canada. The wildlife and native people of the land there have helped me to formulate my own inner spirituality. . . . To be a nurse in a female-dominated profession and leave it to enter a male-dominated profession such as nature photography presents a challenge. I like it. That is the basis to my life—I seek that which I enjoy and forge ahead."

NANCY WEBB
Born May 3, 1944, in Hinton, West Virginia.
Nancy's work has been responsible in part for the proposed protection of 63,000 acres of Louisiana's cypress swamps. "I hope I can reach people with my pictures and make them more aware of things they pass or walk over every day. There has to be more respect for life, no matter how small. What I do is just my share of saving the environment. It's Louisiana's natural heritage, and what would we have left without it?"

PUBLISHER ACKNOWLEDGEMENTS

The editor is grateful to the following publishers and copyright holders for permission to use the selections reprinted in this book.

Diane Ackerman, *A Natural History of the Senses*. Copyright © 1990 by Diane Ackerman. Reprinted by permission of Random House, Inc.

Diane Ackerman, "A Reporter at Large: Penguins," *The New Yorker Magazine*, July 10, 1989. Reprinted by permission of The New Yorker Magazine.

Diane Ackerman, "A Reporter at Large: Albatrosses," *The New Yorker Magazine*, September 24, 1990. Reprinted by permission of The New Yorker Magazine.

Paula Gunn Allen, *The Sacred Hoop*. Copyright © 1986 by Paula Gunn Allen. Reprinted by permission of Beacon Press, Boston.

Hildegard of Bingen, *Meditations with Hildegard of Bingen* by Gabriel Uhlein. Copyright © 1983 Bear & Co., Inc. Reprinted by permission of Bear & Co., Inc., P.O. Drawer 2860, Santa Fe, NM 87504.

Margaret Bourke-White, quoted in *The Woman's Eye*, by Anne Tucker. Copyright © 1973. Reprinted by permission of the Bourke-White Estate.

Anne Cameron, "Orca's Child," from *Dzelarhons: Mythology of the Northwest Coast*. Copyright © 1986 by Anne Cameron. Reprinted by permission of Harbour Publishing.

Rachel Carson, *Silent Spring*. Copyright © 1962 by Rachel L. Carson. Reprinted by permission of Houghton Mifflin Company. All rights reserved.

Rachel Carson, *A Sense of Wonder*. Copyright © 1956 by Rachel L. Carson. Copyright renewed 1984 by Roger Christie. Reprinted by permission of HarperCollins Publishers.

Lois Crisler, *Arctic Wild*. Copyright © 1958 by Lois Crisler. Reprinted by permission of HarperCollins Publishers.

Gilean Davis, *Silence is My Homeland*. Harrisburg, PA: Stackpole Books, 1978. Reprinted by permission of Stackpole Books.

Agnes DeMille, "Do I Hear A Waltz?," *The New York Times Magazine*, May 11, 1975. Reprinted by permission of Agnes DeMille.

Annie Dillard, *Pilgrim at Tinker Creek*. Copyright © 1974 by Annie Dillard. Reprinted by permission of HarperCollins Publishers.

Isak Dineson, "The Deluge at Norderney," *Seven Gothic Tales*. Reprinted by permission of Random House, Inc.

Gretel Ehrlich, from 1989 *Wilderness Wall Calendar* Introduction "River History." Reprinted by permission of Sierra Club Books.

Gretel Ehrlich, *The Solace of Open Spaces*. Copyright © 1985 by Gretel Ehrlich. Reprinted by permission of Viking Penguin, a division of Penguin Books USA, Inc.

Virginia Eifert, *Land of the Snowshoe Hare*. Dodd, Mead, and Co., 1961. Reprinted by permission of Larry Eifert.

Hildegard Flanner, "The Old Cherry Tree," *Brief Cherishing: A Napa Valley Harvest*. Copyright © 1985 by Hildegard Flanner. Reprinted with permission of John Daniel and Company, Publishers.

Elizabeth Dodson Gray, "Turning to Another Way," from *Green Paradise Lost*. Copyright © 1979 by Elizabeth Dodson Gray. Reprinted by permission of Roundtable Press.

Susan Griffin, *Woman and Nature: The Roaring Inside Her*. Copyright © 1978 by Susan Griffin. Reprinted by permission of HarperCollins Publishers.

H.D., *Collected Poems 1912-1944*. Copyright © 1982 by the estate of Hilda Doolittle. Reprinted by permission of New Directions Publishing Corporation.

Linda Hogan, "Waking up the Rake," *Parabola: The Magazine of Myth and Tradition*, Vol. XIII, No. 3. (Summer 1988). Reprinted by permission of Linda Hogan.

Patricia Hubbell, "Prayer for Reptiles," from *8 A.M. Shadows*. Copyright © 1965 by Patricia Hubbell. Reprinted with the permission of Atheneum Publishers, an imprint of Macmillan Publishing Company.

Sue Hubbell, *A Country Year: Living the Questions*. Copyright © 1986 by Sue Hubbell. Reprinted by permission of Random House, Inc.

Cathy Johnson, *On Becoming Lost: A Naturalist's Search for Meaning*. 1990, Gibbs Smith, Publisher/Peregrine Smith Books.

Dolores LaChapelle, *Sacred Land Sacred Sex Rapture of the Deep: Concerning Deep Ecology and Celebrating Life*. Silverton, CO: Finn Hill Arts, 1988.

Gayle D. Lauradunn, "What the Ancient Ones Knew." By permission of the author.

Anne Morrow Lindbergh, *Gift from the Sea*. Copyright © 1955 by Anne Morrow Lindbergh. Reprinted by permission of Pantheon Books, a division of Random House, Inc.

Joan McIntyre, *Mind in the Waters: A Book to Celebrate the Consciousness of Whales and Dolphins*. Copyright © 1974. Reprinted with permission of Sierra Club Books.

Joanna Macy, "Our Life as Gaia," *Thinking Like a Mountain: Towards A Council of All Beings* by John Seed, Joanna Macy *et al*. New Society Publishers, Philadelphia and Gabriola Island.

Julian of Norwich, *Meditations with Julian of Norwich* edited by Brendan Doyle. Copyright © 1983 Bear & Co. Reprinted with permission of Bear & Co., Inc. P.O. Drawer 2860, Santa Fe, NM 87504.

Joyce Carol Oates, "Against Nature," from *On Nature*, edited by Daniel Halpern, North Point Press, 1987. Copyright © 1987 by the Ontario Review, Inc. Reprinted by permission of John Hawkins and Associates, Inc.

Jean Pearson, "A Daily Prayer," from *On Speaking Terms with Earth*. Copyright © 1987 by Jean Pearson. Originally published by Great Elm Press, 1988; reissued by Green World Press, 1993. Reprinted by permission of the author.

Brenda Peterson, *Living by Water: Essays on Life, Land & Spirit*. Copyright © 1990 by Brenda Peterson. Reprinted with permission of Alaska Northwest Books,™ an imprint of Graphic Arts Center Publishing Co., P.O. Box 10306, Portland, OR 97210.

Dorothy Richards with Hope Sawyer Buyukmihci, *Beaversprite: My Years Building an Animal Sanctuary*. Copyright © 1977 by Dorothy Richards. Reprinted by permission of Chronicle Books, San Francisco.

Grace Gallatin Seton, *The Singing Traveler*, published by The Christopher Publishing House, Boston. Copyright 1947 by the Estate of Grace Gallatin Seton.

Ntozake Shange, *Sassafras, Cypress Indigo*, St. Martin's Press, Inc., New York, NY 1982. © 1982 by Ntozake Shange. Reprinted by permission of St. Martin's Press, Inc., New York, NY.

Leslie Marmon Silko, "Landscape, History, and the Pueblo Imagination," from *On Nature*, edited by Daniel Halpern, North Point Press, 1987. Copyright © 1987 by Leslie Marmon Silko. Reprinted by permission of Wylie, Aitken & Stone, Inc.

Eunice Tietjens, "The Most-Sacred Mountain." From *The Home Book of Modern Verse*, edited by Burton Egbert Stevenson, 1965 edition. Reprinted by permission of daughter Janet Hart and son Marshall Head.

Alice Walker, "The Universe Responds: Or, How I Learned We Can Have Peace on Earth," from *Living By the Word*. Copyright © 1987 by Alice Walker. Reprinted by permission of Harcourt Brace Jovanovich, Inc.

Alice Walker, "We Have a Beautiful Mother," from *Her Blue Body Everything We Know*. Copyright © 1991 by Alice Walker, reprinted by permission of Harcourt Brace Jovanovich, Inc.

Opal Whiteley, *The Singing Creek Where the Willows Grow: The Rediscovered Diary of Opal Whiteley*, presented by Benjamin Hoff. Ticknor & Fields, New York, 1986. Presentation copyright © 1986 by Benjamin Hoff. Reprinted by permission of Benjamin Hoff.

Ruth Yarrow, *A Journal for Reflections, Poems*. Copyright © 1988 by Ruth Yarrow, published by The Crossing Press, Freedom, California 95019.

Ann Zwinger, *Wind in the Rock*. Copyright © 1978 by Ann H. Zwinger. Reprinted by permission of HarperCollins Publishers.

Ann Zwinger, *The Mysterious Lands*. Copyright © 1989 by Ann Haymond Zwinger. Used by permission of the publisher, Dutton, an imprint of New American Library, a division of Penguin Books USA, Inc.